EveryDay Feasts

SECOND IN THE SERIES

FROM

THE JUNIOR LEAGUE OF TAMPA

CULINARY COLLECTION

JUNIOR
LEAGUE
of TAMPA
*Culinary
Collection*

CREATORS OF

THE GASPARILLA COOKBOOK, A TASTE OF TAMPA, TAMPA TREASURES,
AND THE LIFE OF THE PARTY

To purchase copies of *EveryDay Feasts*, visit us online at www.jltampa.org, complete
the order form in the back of this book, or call The Junior League of Tampa at 813-254-1734, extension 502.

FROM OUR TABLE

Welcome to *EveryDay Feasts*, the second book in The Junior League of Tampa's Culinary Collection. Inspired by the continuing challenges families face to create memorable meals, *EveryDay Feasts* is a tribute to the diversity of families and a celebration of the role that food plays in gathering people together. We welcome you into our homes and encourage you to taste and enjoy what we bring to the table.

Fresh ingredients, big flavor, quick preparation—we believe that food should be an experience that will awaken your senses, remind you of a special time, and create new memories that will stay with you and those you love. We feel that any gathering can be cause for celebration—large or small, simple or elaborate. We hope our Weeknight Wonders menu will inspire your family to fit delicious food into any day, no matter how hectic. In Treasured Traditions, you'll be taken back to a day when the family table was the mainstay of communication, and we'll give you ideas to help create your own traditions and rituals. Reservations for Sunset reminds us that you can choose to have a gourmet romantic dinner without ever leaving your home. And Portable Fare emphasizes how food is still the bond that connects even beyond your immediate family.

Good food can be a treasured gift from the heart, a link to the past, and an opportunity to share a new experience. So please come in and have a seat at our table. We hope you'll enjoy reading and using this book to discover new ways to connect with your friends, family, and community.

—*EveryDay Feasts Committee*

EveryDay Feasts

THE JUNIOR LEAGUE OF TAMPA
Culinary Collection

EveryDay Feasts

Volume 2 of The Junior League of Tampa Culinary Collection

The Junior League of Tampa, Inc., is an organization of women committed to promoting voluntarism, developing the potential of women, and improving communities through effective action and leadership of trained volunteers. Its purpose is exclusively educational and charitable.

Proceeds from the sale of this cookbook will be reinvested in the community through Junior League of Tampa projects.

The Junior League of Tampa, Inc.
87 Columbia Drive
Tampa, Florida 33606
813-254-1734

Copyright 2005 by
The Junior League of Tampa, Inc.

ISBN: 0-9609556-4-X
Library of Congress Control Number: 2004104554

Edited, Designed and Manufactured by
Favorite Recipes Press

FRP™

P.O. Box 305142
Nashville, Tennessee 37230
800-358-0560

Book Design: David Malone
Art Director: Steve Newman
Project Manager: Tanis Westbrook

Manufactured in the United States of America
First Printing 2005
20,000 copies

This cookbook is a collection of favorite recipes, which are not necessarily original recipes.

MAJOR CONTRIBUTORS

Special thanks to our major contributors for their gracious support of *EVERYDAY FEASTS*.

FRONT COVER SPONSOR—Mary Lee Nunnally Farrior
BACK COVER SPONSOR—Laura Mickler Bentley
CORPORATE SPONSOR—Horizon Bay Senior Communities

COOKBOOK PHOTOGRAPHY—Robert Adamo
FOOD STYLIST—Kristie Salzer
FLORIST—The Arrangement Florist, Louis and Carol Radwanski
THE JUNIOR LEAGUE OF TAMPA CULINARY COLLECTION LOGO—
Atlas Advertising and Design, Christy Atlas

COOKBOOK DEVELOPMENT COMMITTEE

CHAIRMAN
Terrie Dodson-Caldevilla

SUSTAINER ADVISOR
Kristie Salzer

COMMUNICATIONS COORDINATOR
Jacque Bordonali

COPYWRITING/EDITING
Kristie Salzer, Danielle Welsh

PHOTOGRAPHY
Kim Harcrow, Paula Perry, Karyn Sbar

RECIPE COLLECTION
Tweed Cline Eckhard, Laura Farrior

RECIPE TESTING
Dianne Rossi, Janice Straske

Susan O'Neal Thompson, President 2004-2005
Lisa Cave Andrews, President 2003-2004

WOMEN BUILDING BETTER COMMUNITIES

 Junior League of Tampa cookbooks have always served as a legacy, an investment of time and tradition, handed from one generation to another, from our community to yours. But more than that, Junior League of Tampa cookbooks are an investment in the foundation of our community.

Since 1926, the volunteers in our organization have shared their time, talent, and treasures with the city of Tampa. Here is a glimpse of some of the projects and organizations that we have been proud to support through volunteer hours and money raised through fund-raisers, including the sale of our cookbooks.

Academy Prep
Adoption Events for Special Needs Children
Alpha House, A Home for Pregnant Women
Baby Bungalow, An Early Childhood Resource and Support Center
Child Abuse Council
Children's Cancer Center
FunBook/FunCart for Hospitalized Children
Guardian Ad Litem
Habitat for Humanity
H. Lee Moffitt Hospital & Cancer Research Institute
Immunization Promotional Campaign
Lifepath Hospice Circle of Love Bereavement Camp
Lowry Park Zoo
Metropolitan Ministries Day Care Center
Minority Youth Leadership Program for Girls
MORE Health, An Educational Program for Schoolchildren
PACE Center for Girls
Recycling Made Easy
Ronald McDonald House
Tampa Bay Performing Arts Center
Tampa General Hospital Sunshine House
The Children's Literacy Project
The Children's Museum of Tampa & Kid City
The Spring of Tampa Bay, A Domestic Violence Shelter
Thumbs Up for Child Safety

Contents

GATHERINGS

LITTLE HELPERS

A love of cooking and food can begin when children are very young. Kids love to be part of the action in the kitchen, and this is a great time to teach them some important and fun lessons about safety, food, and nutrition.

CONSIDER THESE THOUGHTS TO HELP MAKE COOKING WITH YOUR LITTLE HELPERS A POSITIVE EXPERIENCE:

MENU

HOT CHOCOLATE WITH WHIPPED CREAM

MORNING GRANOLA WITH FRESH BERRIES

TUSCAN FRITTATA

CARROT BREAD

DOUBLE APPLE MUFFINS

a recipe with your child and setting up your ingredients ahead of time.

- It's a good idea to have items sliced or chopped before a child is invited to join you. Younger children can help wash vegetables, set the table, make decorations, mash things, "paint" butter or oil in pans, and sprinkle cheese or other toppings.

- Insist that helpers wash their hands prior to starting and that an adult always be present while cooking.
- Keep the other rules simple so the child will have a positive, fun experience.
- Baking is a safe place to start because it doesn't require knives and uses simple ingredients.
- Assign tasks that children can do themselves rather than just being shown.
- Set up a workstation where a child can comfortably see ingredients and the inside of pans.
- Create good habits by always reading through

STILL NOT SURE IF YOU'RE UP TO THE CHALLENGE OF KIDS IN THE KITCHEN? CONSIDER WHAT CHILDREN GAIN FROM COOKING:

- creativity
- confidence and self-esteem
- a sense that "I can do it!"
- math and reading skills
- organizational skills
- teamwork
- observation of science in action
- patience and a sense of time
- interest and curiosity about new foods

WEEKNIGHT WONDERS

MENU

BLUE CHEESE AND CHIVE SPREAD WITH CRUDITÉS

LEMON CAPER SHRIMP WITH ORZO

GARLIC GREEN BEANS

CRUSTY BREAD

APPLE CLAFOUTI

In that age-old quest for great taste, satisfaction, and empty plates in our everyday meals, does food become the sacrifice you make to try to gain more time? Does the usual weekday five o'clock dash—carpools in and out, spouses working late, cries for help with homework—find you asking, "What's for dinner?"

With a little planning and advance preparation time, weeknight meals do not have to mean drive-through windows. Entice your family to the table with recipes that give you home-cooked flavor with the convenience of take-out.

INCORPORATE THESE SIMPLE SUGGESTIONS TO HELP YOU PLAN WEEKNIGHT MEALS:

• Have a few good marinade recipes on hand. Just place your meat or fish and the marinade in a freezer bag and freeze. Remove when you're ready to use it, and place it in the refrigerator in the morning.

It will marinate while it defrosts, and you've got the mainstay of your meal ready for the grill or oven that evening.

• Slow cookers can be a cook's best friend when you're short on time. How can you resist putting your ingredients in one pot, flipping the switch, and coming home to the savory aroma of a soul-warming soup or entrée?

• Planned meals don't necessarily mean cooking every night. Leftover fish, pork, or chicken can be used to create a main dish salad or quick pasta the next day with little effort.

• Use recipes that incorporate shortcuts, don't take long to put together, or can be pulled out of the freezer and presented in no time.

• Take a few minutes on a weekend to make menus and a grocery list for three or four weeknight meals. You'll be more likely to cook meals if you can avoid daily trips to the market.

MEET YOUR NEIGHBORS

Nothing says all-American like the neighborhood gatherings of our youth. Our need to connect as a family, group, or community goes as far back as time itself. Whether it's a family reunion or an opportunity to congregate with neighbors, food is a universal expression of camaraderie and friendship.

Organizing a neighborhood or family event can seem like a daunting task, but with careful preparation and many helping hands, the load can be easily lightened.

HERE ARE SOME IDEAS TO CONSIDER WHEN GATHERING THE MULTITUDES:

- Promote a neighborhood event by creating fun, informative flyers. Get the kids involved by letting them deliver newsletters to families on each block.
- Anticipate your needs and order your party essentials like tables and tablecloths, chairs, plates, and utensils ahead of time.

MENU

RED ROCKETS

SUMMER VEGETABLE CROSTINI

TRIO OF ROASTED PEPPERS

SEAFOOD GUMBO

MIXED GREENS WITH BALSAMIC VINAIGRETTE

MASCARPONE FRUIT TART

SUGAR COOKIES

- If you have plenty of name tags and pens available when everybody arrives, neighbors can get to know each other easily.
- Do you have a neighbor with a recipe for the best pie? Find out if people have a specialty and seek them out to make it. Then plan other items to ensure a good variety.
- Remember that taste buds vary. Whether you have children and adults or just adults, not everyone eats everything, so consider an array of foods.
- Keep in mind that people eat meats and starches more than vegetables at parties.
- Nostalgia is an important part of community gatherings. Do you have fond memories of turning the crank on an ice cream maker and waiting for that first taste? Remember the lemonade popsicles made in ice-cube trays that you shared with your next-door neighbors? Incorporate some feel-good memories of your own into your food by creating something your children will remember.

Outdoor Feasts

There is a simple pleasure in enjoying your food in the great outdoors. If weather permits, the back porch or poolside makes any ordinary meal a little more special. The sunshine can make your foods more vibrant, give an enticing sheen to a cold drink, and infuse energy into the meal.

The grill is a great component of outdoor meals because any variety of meats and seafood can be cooked on it, even most vegetables and some fruits. You'll want to always have a backup plan for weather that doesn't cooperate, or unwanted guests like mosquitoes, but why not make the most of nature for your next meal?

• The outdoors is a great venue for self-serve food. Set it up buffet style, and watch it disappear.

MENU

ICED LEMONADE WITH
VODKA AND MINT

BRIE WITH HERBS IN BAGUETTE

TRIO OF WRAPS:
GRILLED FLANK STEAK,
MEDITERRANEAN AND CUBAN

SWEET CORN AND PEPPER SALAD

FRESH CARROT SALAD

PEACH POUND CAKE WITH
OLD-FASHIONED VANILLA ICE CREAM

• Simplicity is the name of the game here. Take the time to prepare food ahead.

• Choose foods that hold up well at room temperature, and keep them light. An arrangement of fresh salads works well.

• What's an outdoor feast without a festive drink?

• If you're taking your food on the road, wraps are an excellent choice for a picnic. They're easy to make ahead, transport, and handle, whether you're sitting at a table or on a blanket.

• When cooking for a crowd, remember that even if a recipe serves six well, it doesn't mean that doubling it to serve twelve will work. If you're not sure that a recipe doubles well, make several batches instead, or find a recipe you are confident can be easily doubled.

RESERVATIONS FOR SUNSET

MENU

MUSHROOM PÂTÉ

FIELD GREENS TOSSED WITH LEMON
DIJON VINAIGRETTE AND CROUTONS

BEEF TENDERLOIN WITH BLUE CHEESE
AND PORT-CARAMELIZED ONIONS

WILD RICE WITH CRANBERRIES
AND ALMONDS

OVEN-ROASTED ASPARAGUS WITH
THYME AND SHALLOT DRESSING

CHOCOLATE TORTE

Soft candlelight. Soothing music. Invigorating smells from a distant kitchen. Sound like a romantic evening out at your favorite restaurant? We've got the scoop on food you can make to create warmth on the inside and out at home.

Charlie Trotter said, *"The art of cooking is among the most intimate things that we can do for one another."* So step outside the box, forget the reservations at the restaurant tonight, and create a night to remember in your own kitchen.

THIS CHECKLIST WILL HELP YOU SPRINKLE SOME ROMANCE INTO YOUR NEXT MEAL AND LEAVE YOUR SPECIAL SOMEONE WONDERING HOW YOU DID IT:

• Choose recipes that you can make ahead as much as possible. Remember that the point of the special meal is to enjoy the company of the one(s) you're with.

• Mix things up— you don't always have to eat at the kitchen or dining room table! Enjoy your meal out on the balcony or the back porch, or dine in front of the fireplace.

• Jazz up a familiar room with fresh flowers and lots of candles.

• Music is a great way to set the tone for an evening. Do you remember what you listened to when you first met? Use the music to recapture special memories.

• We give you some fun menus to play with, but use your memory as your guide, and re-create a memorable meal you shared on some long-ago occasion, like a first date.

TREASURED TRADITIONS

To many, the family meal is the central point of communication within a family.

Family traditions and rituals bind us together, marking milestones and the passage of time. Most often remembered during the holidays, traditions can be a way to bring family and friends together throughout the year.

Celebrations provide an opportunity to pass on many childhood memories, histories, and values to another generation. They can be simple or elaborate, casual or dressy—they are as varied as the families that create them. The way you "do" something becomes the special tradition that is created to mark an occasion. The most important component is being together and having fun.

A good way to start is to ask your family members what they most enjoyed doing during the last year. That way, you will have an idea of what to repeat.

MENU
APPLE GINGER FIZZ

CREAMY RED ONION SOUP

SALTIMBOCCA

ZUCCHINI SAUTÉ

CHERRY TOMATOES PROVENÇAL

VANILLA LAYER CAKE WITH BUTTER CREAM ICING

HERE ARE SOME IDEAS FOR CREATING OR ADDING TO YOUR OWN TRADITIONS:

• Have a family dinner at least once a week. Set the table, and take time to enjoy a meal. Share the day's or week's "highs" and "lows." Celebrate a great report card, a new job, or the completion of a big project. Let the honored person eat on a special plate.

• Treat the birthday boy or girl to breakfast in bed, a special lunch, or the homemade dinner of their choice. Donate a book or gift to an area shelter or library in the child's name to commemorate the day.

• Children love to learn about their parents' childhoods. Invite grandparents, aunts, uncles, and cousins over to watch old home movies. Turn off the lights, pop popcorn, and reminisce together.

• Set aside Saturday or Sunday morning as family time. Treat yourselves to a big breakfast and lazy time together.

PORTABLE FARE

MENU

ROASTED VEGETABLE SOUP

SPINACH SALAD WITH APPLES
AND MANCHEGO CHEESE

GRILLED CHICKEN BROCHETTES

LEMON RICE

MILK CHOCOLATE
MACADAMIA NUT COOKIES

There is something so innately comforting about a home-cooked meal—whether you're the cook or the fortunate recipient of the meal. Poet Maya Angelou wrote, "*I have found that among its other benefits, giving liberates the soul of the giver.*" For decades, in instances of grief, the joyful arrival of babies, families faced with trauma or illness, or just the expression of celebration, the gift of food has had the ability to create powerful sentiments.

WE HOPE OUR TIPS HELP YOU TAKE YOUR MEAL OR TREAT ON THE ROAD WITH EASE AS WELL AS STYLE:

• By doubling what you are preparing for your family, you can easily package the extra for someone else to enjoy. Be sure to ask what your friend or neighbor likes to eat so you can include some comforting favorites. At the same time, you want to be sensitive to food allergies or dietary constraints.

• Display your food gift in different ways to make the gift even more memorable. Line a basket with a colorful dish towel or napkin. Use festive containers or dishes from party stores. Place soup in a glass jar and tie raffia around the top. Place cookies, breads, or rolls in a cellophane bag with a ribbon tied around them, and tuck in some fresh flowers.

• Label food with colorful tags that include heating instructions and freezing information if it is something that can be enjoyed later.

• Consider using a disposable container. If you prefer taking a nondisposable utensil, make sure you label it so you can easily retrieve it later.

• Don't let the idea that you have to create a whole meal stop you from cooking for someone. The smallest gesture will elicit sincere appreciation from a sleep-deprived new mom or an elderly neighbor recuperating from surgery. A jar of warm soup or a sweet treat will go a long way in helping someone feel cared for and loved.

STARTERS

SPINACH SALAD WITH APPLES AND MANCHEGO CHEESE

This is a wonderful combination of spicy, sweet, and savory in a salad dish. The flavors blend well. Manchego is a dry, semi-sharp cheese that is similar to Cheddar.

1/4 cup balsamic vinegar
1/4 cup high quality Grade A
maple syrup
1/4 cup olive oil
Salt and pepper to taste
2 (6-ounce) packages baby spinach

2 large Granny Smith apples,
halved and thinly sliced
4 ounces manchego cheese,
shaved
1/2 cup Spicy Salad Nuts (below)

Combine the vinegar, syrup and olive oil in a small bowl and whisk until blended. Season with salt and pepper and set aside. Combine the spinach, apples, cheese and Spicy Salad Nuts in a large bowl. Drizzle with the dressing and toss to coat. You may prepare the dressing up to 1 day in advance. Store in the refrigerator until ready to serve.

Yield: 8 servings

SPICY SALAD NUTS

Melt 2 tablespoons butter in a small skillet over medium to medium-high heat. Add 2 tablespoons sugar and 1/4 teaspoon each cayenne pepper and salt and mix well. Stir in 1 cup sliced almonds, chopped pecans or chopped walnuts. Cook until the nuts begin to brown, stirring constantly. Spread the nuts on a tray covered with waxed paper. Chill in the refrigerator until set. Sprinkle over salads with dried fruit, fresh berries, goat cheese or blue cheese. Store, tightly covered, in the refrigerator for up to 1 week or freeze in a sealable plastic bag for up to 1 month. Yield: 1 cup.

BRIE AND APRICOT PHYLLO BITES

These simple yet impressive canapés won rave reviews at our tasting events.
They pair well with brunch menus or cocktails.

1 (8-ounce) wedge Brie cheese,
   rind removed
30 frozen phyllo shells
1/2 cup (1 stick) butter, melted

2/3 cup apricot preserves
2 cups fresh or dried apricots,
   finely chopped
1/4 to 1/2 cup sliced almonds, or to taste

Preheat the oven to 350 degrees. Cut the Brie into thirty 1/2-inch cubes. Arrange the phyllo shells on a baking sheet. Brush the phyllo shells with the butter. Bake for 5 minutes. Remove from the oven and let cool on the baking sheet. Spoon 1 teaspoon of the apricot preserves into each shell. Place a piece of the Brie in each prepared shell. Top with a small amount of the apricots and sprinkle with the almonds. Bake for 5 to 10 minutes or until the Brie is melted and beginning to brown. Serve warm.

Yield: 30 appetizers

BRIE WITH HERBS IN A BAGUETTE

3 tablespoons dry white wine
2 fresh garlic cloves, mashed
1 teaspoon freshly ground pepper
1/4 cup extra-virgin olive oil
1 French baguette
1/4 cup fresh thyme, stemmed

1 cup coarsely chopped
   fresh basil leaves
3 tablespoons finely chopped
   fresh chives
16 ounces Brie cheese, rind
   removed

Combine the wine, garlic and pepper in a bowl and mix well. Whisk in the olive oil until blended. Let stand for 30 minutes to several hours. Cut the baguette in half lengthwise. Combine the thyme, basil and chives in a small bowl. Cut the Brie into 1/8-inch slices. Drizzle the cut sides of the baguette with the olive oil mixture. Sprinkle half the herb mixture over 1 of the prepared baguette halves. Top with the Brie and sprinkle with the remaining herb mixture. Top with the remaining baguette half. Wrap tightly with plastic wrap and foil. Place between 2 baking sheets and top with a heavy weight. Chill for 5 to 8 hours. To serve, remove the foil and plastic wrap and cut into 1-inch slices.

Yield: 16 slices

SUMMER VEGETABLE CROSTINI

This makes a festive, healthful appetizer or a light entrée when tossed with pasta.

2 Roma tomatoes, seeded and finely chopped
2 yellow squash, finely chopped
1 zucchini, finely chopped
2/3 cup finely chopped red onion
2 tablespoons finely chopped oil-packed sun-dried tomatoes
2 tablespoons capers, drained

2 teaspoons minced fresh garlic
2 tablespoons white wine vinegar
2 tablespoons olive oil
1/2 to 1 teaspoon red pepper flakes
1/2 teaspoon salt
1/4 teaspoon freshly ground black pepper
1/2 teaspoon sugar

Combine the Roma tomatoes, yellow squash, zucchini, red onion, sun-dried tomatoes, capers and garlic in a large bowl; set aside. Combine the vinegar, olive oil, red pepper, salt, black pepper and sugar in a small bowl and whisk until blended. Pour the vinaigrette over the vegetable mixture and mix gently. Serve over crostini. This may be served immediately or chilled for up to 4 days.

Yield: 1 quart

CROSTINI

Preheat the broiler. Cut 1 French baguette into 1/4- to 1/2-inch slices. Spread both sides of each baguette slice with butter and arrange on a baking sheet. Broil until light golden brown. Turn the baguette slices over and broil until golden brown. Remove from the oven and let stand until cool. These may be stored for up to 2 days. Yield: 2 to 3 dozen crostini.

TRIO OF ROASTED PEPPERS

Bright roasted peppers surrounded by fresh mozzarella cheese, artichoke hearts, olives,
and hearts of palm make a delightful menu addition for a casual gathering, whether they
are served as a prelude to a meal or as a side dish.

2 yellow bell peppers, seeded, cored and quartered
2 red bell peppers, seeded, cored and quartered
2 orange bell peppers, seeded, cored and quartered
5 fresh garlic cloves, minced
1/4 cup extra-virgin olive oil
1/2 teaspoon balsamic vinegar
2 tablespoons capers, drained
Salt to taste

Preheat the broiler. Arrange the bell peppers skin side up on a baking sheet lined with foil. Broil until the bell peppers are black and charred. Remove from the oven and place the peppers in a paper bag or large plastic container with an airtight lid. Let stand for 20 minutes or longer. Run the bell peppers under cold water and remove the skins. Combine with the garlic, olive oil, vinegar, capers and salt in a large bowl and toss to coat. Arrange the bell peppers on a serving platter.

Yield: about 2 cups

BASIC HERB VINEGAR

Heat vinegar of your choice in a saucepan. Do not boil.

Pour into a bottle and add 1 or more herbs of your choice.

Seal tightly and let stand for 2 weeks before using.

ROASTED BAR NUTS

One handful of these delicious nuts won't be enough! Keep them on hand in your freezer for last-minute entertaining.

1 pound your favorite mixed nuts, such as peanuts,
hazelnuts, walnuts, pecans and almonds
2 tablespoons butter, melted
1 tablespoon dark brown sugar
1 tablespoon chopped fresh rosemary
1 teaspoon kosher salt
1 teaspoon cayenne pepper

Preheat the oven to 350 degrees. Spread the nuts on a baking sheet. Bake for 10 minutes or until toasted. Combine the butter, brown sugar, rosemary, kosher salt and cayenne pepper in a bowl and mix well. Add the nuts and toss to coat. Serve warm. You may freeze the nuts. Warm briefly in the oven or microwave before serving.

Yield: about 3 cups

GARLIC CHEESE SPREAD

This is an attractive and easy spread that can be made ahead.

8 ounces extra-sharp white Cheddar
cheese, shredded
1 bunch scallions, bulbs and tops chopped
1/2 teaspoon garlic salt or to taste
1/2 cup mayonnaise

Combine the cheese, scallions, garlic salt and mayonnaise in a bowl and stir gently, adding additional mayonnaise if necessary to bind the mixture. Serve with thin wheat crackers.

Yield: about 2 cups

MUSHROOM PÂTÉ

We love this make-ahead hors d'oeuvre! Its ingredients are readily available,
and it is simple to assemble.

8 ounces mushrooms, sliced
2 tablespoons butter
1/2 cup finely chopped scallion bulbs
11/2 teaspoons finely chopped fresh garlic
1/3 cup chicken broth
2 tablespoons butter, softened
4 ounces cream cheese, softened
2 tablespoons finely chopped scallion tops
Salt and pepper to taste
1 to 2 scallions, finely chopped

Chop the mushrooms in a food processor by pulsing 3 or 4 times. Melt 2 tablespoons butter in a large skillet over high heat. Add the mushrooms and sauté for 2 minutes or until darkened. Add the scallion bulbs and garlic and cook for 1 minute. Add the chicken broth and cook for 3 to 5 minutes or until the liquid evaporates, stirring frequently.

Remove the mixture from the heat and let cool slightly. Add 2 tablespoons butter and the cream cheese and mix well. Stir in the scallion tops and season with salt and pepper. Spoon into a serving dish. Chill, covered, for 8 hours or longer. Let stand at room temperature for 30 minutes to 1 hour before serving. Garnish with chopped scallions and serve with water crackers.

Yield: 11/2 cups

GREEN OLIVE TAPENADE

This tapenade is a terrific "basic" to have available. It doubles as a topping for grilled chicken breasts. You may add more nuts or garlic to suit your taste.

4 to 5 ounces fresh Parmesan
  cheese, shredded
1 (13-ounce) jar pimento-stuffed
  green olives, drained
1 bunch parsley, stemmed

4 fresh garlic cloves
1/4 to 1/2 cup pine nuts or
  walnuts
Olive oil
Salt and pepper to taste

Combine the Parmesan cheese, olives, parsley, garlic and pine nuts in a food processor and pulse until minced. Spoon the mixture into a bowl and stir in enough olive oil to bind. Season with salt and pepper. Serve with crackers or crostini. This may be chilled, tightly covered, for up to 1 week.

Yield: about 2 cups

CARAMELIZED ONION DIP

This updated version of an old favorite will be devoured before halftime by your friends and family.

1 cup Slow-Cooked Onions
  (page 52)
1/2 cup mayonnaise
1/2 cup sour cream
2 tablespoons cream cheese
1/4 to 1/2 teaspoon salt

1/4 to 1/2 teaspoon cayenne
  pepper
1/2 teaspoon crushed red pepper
1/2 cup Slow-Cooked Onions
  (page 52)

Combine 1 cup onions, mayonnaise, sour cream, cream cheese, salt, cayenne pepper and red pepper in a food processor fitted with a steel blade and process until smooth. Spoon into a bowl. Fold in the remaining 1/2 cup onions. Chill, covered, until ready to serve. Serve with crackers, potato chips or crudités.

Yield: 1 1/2 cups

BLUE CHEESE AND CHIVE DIP

Our testers said this dip was the perfect thing to snack on while preparing dinner. It can be accompanied by crudités, sliced fruit, or crackers and keeps in the refrigerator for up to one week.

4 ounces cream cheese, softened
2 ounces crumbled blue cheese
2 tablespoons sour cream
3 tablespoons dry white wine
2 ounces crumbled blue cheese
1 tablespoon finely chopped fresh chives
Dash of Tabasco sauce (optional)

Combine the cream cheese, 2 ounces blue cheese, the sour cream and wine in a blender or food processor fitted with a steel blade and process until smooth. Spoon into a bowl. Stir in 2 ounces blue cheese, the chives and Tabasco sauce. Serve with vegetables, apple and pear slices or crackers.

Yield: 1¹/2 cups

PITA TRIANGLES

Preheat the oven to 350 degrees. Cut 6 pita rounds into 8 wedges each. Separate each wedge into 2 pieces. Brush lightly with melted unsalted butter and place on a baking sheet. Sprinkle lightly with garlic salt and shredded Parmesan cheese. Bake for 10 minutes, checking frequently to make sure that the chips do not brown too quickly. Remove from the oven and let stand until cool. These may be served immediately or stored for up to 5 days. Yield: about 8 dozen chips.

CORN CHOWDER

Enjoy this rich chowder with a green salad and bread for a hearty lunch or savory supper. A great way to use fresh corn when it is readily available.

5 strips bacon, cut into
1/2-inch pieces
2 tablespoons unsalted butter
2 cups chopped onions
2 tablespoons flour
4 cups chicken broth

2 large potatoes, peeled
and diced
1 cup half-and-half
4 cups fresh corn
Salt and pepper to taste

Cook the bacon in a large stockpot over low heat until wilted and the fat is rendered. Add the butter and cook until the butter is melted. Add the onions and sauté for 10 minutes or until translucent. Add the flour and mix well. Cook for 5 minutes, stirring occasionally.

Add the chicken broth and potatoes. Increase the heat to medium and cook for 10 to 15 minutes or just until the potatoes are tender. Stir in the half-and-half, corn and salt and pepper. Cook for 10 minutes, stirring occasionally. You may add 1 cup chopped cooked chicken or 1 (8-ounce) container cleaned fresh crabmeat and a dash of Tabasco sauce and cook just until warmed through.

Yield: 6 to 8 servings

"No one who cooks, cooks alone. Even at her most solitary,

a cook in the kitchen is surrounded by generations

of cooks past, the advice and menus of cooks present,

the wisdom of cookbook writers."

—Laurie Colwin

ITALIAN SAUSAGE SOUP WITH TORTELLINI

A hearty entrée soup that feeds a crowd, this dish is perfect for a post-game meal.

1 pound Italian sausage, casings removed
1 cup coarsely chopped onion
2 fresh garlic cloves, thinly sliced
5 cups beef broth
1/2 cup water
1/2 cup dry red wine
1 (28-ounce) can diced tomatoes
1 (8-ounce) can tomato sauce
1 cup chopped fresh spinach
1/2 teaspoon dried basil
1/2 teaspoon dried oregano
1 1/2 cups sliced zucchini
8 ounces fresh meat- or cheese-filled tortellini
3 tablespoons chopped fresh parsley
1/2 cup shredded fresh Parmesan cheese

Brown the sausage in a 5-quart Dutch oven over medium heat, stirring until crumbly. Remove the sausage with a slotted spoon to a bowl, discarding all but enough of the drippings to coat the bottom of the pan. Sauté the onions and garlic in the drippings until tender. Add the sausage, beef broth, water, wine, undrained tomatoes, tomato sauce, spinach, basil and oregano and mix well. Bring the mixture to a boil, stirring occasionally. Reduce the heat and simmer for 30 minutes, stirring occasionally. Stir in the zucchini, tortellini and parsley. Simmer, covered, for 20 to 25 minutes or until the tortellini is tender. Spoon into soup bowls and sprinkle with Parmesan cheese.

Yield: eight 1 1/2-cup servings

CREAMY RED ONION SOUP

This unique soup is truly special. Its rich flavor and aroma make it a wintertime favorite.

1/4 cup (1/2 stick) butter
3 large red onions, thinly sliced
1/4 cup flour
2 (15-ounce) cans beef broth
1/2 cup dry red wine or sherry
1/2 teaspoon sugar
2 cups half-and-half
Salt and pepper to taste
4 to 6 slices French bread
Crumbled blue cheese
Toasted chopped walnuts

Melt the butter in a Dutch oven over medium-high heat. Add the onions and cook just until caramel-colored, stirring frequently. Reduce the heat to low. Add the flour and mix well. Cook for 1 minute, stirring constantly. Add the broth, wine and sugar gradually, stirring constantly. Cook over medium heat until the mixture is thickened and bubbly, stirring constantly. Stir in the half-and-half and salt and pepper. Cook until heated through, stirring constantly. Ladle into soup bowls. Sprinkle the bread with blue cheese and walnuts and toast the bread. Top the soup with the toasted bread.

Yield: eight 1/2-cup servings

"Happy and successful cooking doesn't rely only on know-how;
it comes from the heart, makes great demands on the palate, and
needs enthusiasm and a great love of food to bring it to life."
—Georges Blanc

TOMATO SOUP

This simple tomato soup is perfect for lunch or a light dinner. Top with goldfish crackers, and serve with grilled cheese sandwiches for younger palates.

6 tablespoons (3/4 stick) butter
2 tablespoons olive oil
1 large onion, thinly sliced
1 teaspoon dried thyme
Salt and pepper to taste
2 1/2 pounds fresh tomatoes, quartered, or
1 (28-ounce) can tomatoes, drained
3 tablespoons tomato paste
1/2 cup flour
3 3/4 cups chicken broth
1 cup heavy cream or milk
1 teaspoon sugar
Basil chiffonade
Garlic croutons (see page 43)

Melt the butter in a large saucepan over low heat. Add the olive oil, onion, thyme and salt and pepper and cook over medium-low heat until the onion is wilted, stirring occasionally. Add the tomatoes and tomato paste and mix well. Increase the heat to medium and simmer for 10 minutes, stirring occasionally.

Combine the flour and 5 tablespoons chicken broth in a small bowl and whisk until blended. Stir into the tomato mixture. Add the remaining broth and simmer for 30 minutes, stirring frequently. Purée the mixture in batches in a food processor. Pour into a saucepan. Stir in the cream and sugar. Cook over low heat for 5 minutes, stirring frequently. Adjust the seasonings to taste. Serve topped with basil chiffonade and garlic croutons.

Chiffonade refers to vegetables or herbs that have been cut into long, thin strips. It is often used as a garnish for soups or salads.

Yield: 4 to 6 servings

ROASTED VEGETABLE SOUP

*This soup is a delicious way to get your vegetables. It is low in fat, and it may
be made ahead and frozen for up to one month.*

2 leeks
6 large tomatoes, sliced in half horizontally
2 large carrots, peeled and cut into 1/2-inch pieces
4 fresh garlic cloves
2 tablespoons olive oil
Salt and pepper to taste
1 quart chicken stock
Basil chiffonade (see page 37)
Crostini or garlic toast

Preheat the oven to 425 degrees. Rinse the leeks in cold water. Cut off the roots and rough tops
of each leek. Rinse in cold water to remove any remaining dirt. Cut the pale green and white parts of
the leeks into 1/2-inch pieces. Place the tomatoes, cut side down, in a large roasting pan. Add the leeks,
carrots and garlic. Drizzle olive oil over the vegetables and sprinkle with salt and pepper. Roast for 40 to
60 minutes or until the carrots are tender, stirring occasionally. Be careful not to let the vegetables
burn. Let stand until cool. Peel the tomatoes.
   Combine the tomatoes with the roasted vegetables in a large saucepan. Add the chicken stock
and mix well. Bring to a simmer over medium heat. Remove from the heat and purée in batches in
a food processor fitted with a steel blade. Ladle into soup bowls. Garnish with basil chiffonade and serve
with crostini or garlic toast.

Yield: 4 to 6 servings

WARM FIG AND PROSCIUTTO SALAD

This delicious fall salad is a treat when fresh figs are in season. The recipe makes a generous amount of dressing that should be used to taste. Store the remaining dressing in the refrigerator for up to one week.

1/2 cup balsamic vinegar
1 cup olive oil
2 tablespoons honey
Salt and pepper to taste
8 fresh figs

1 (4- to 5-ounce) wedge of
Parmesan cheese
8 thin slices prosciutto
4 to 6 ounces field greens

Preheat the oven to 350 degrees. Combine the vinegar, olive oil and honey in a small bowl and whisk until blended. Season with salt and pepper and set aside. Cut the figs in half lengthwise. Shave the Parmesan cheese into 16 very thin slices using a cheese slicer. Cut the prosciutto slices in half lengthwise. Wrap each fig half with a slice of cheese and a slice of prosciutto and place on a baking sheet. Spoon 1 to 2 teaspoons of the dressing over each wrapped fig. Bake for 10 minutes.

Toss the field greens with the dressing to taste. Divide the field greens among 4 to 6 serving plates. Top each with 1 to 3 prepared figs and serve immediately.

Yield: 4 to 6 servings

BALSAMIC VINEGAR SYRUP

Bring 2 cups good quality balsamic vinegar to a slow boil in a medium saucepan over medium-high heat. Reduce the heat to medium and cook for 20 minutes or until reduced by 2/3 and syrupy, stirring frequently. Serve over chèvre cheese or sliced fresh tomatoes and Buffalo mozzarella cheese, or drizzle over grilled vegetables or meats. Store in the refrigerator for up to 1 week.

REALLY GOOD CHICKEN SALAD

What makes chicken salad taste so good is simple and fresh ingredients. Serve this over lettuce leaves for a lunch meeting, or stuff into rolls for a tasty brown-bag treat.

3 chicken breasts, poached and chopped (see below)
2 to 3 ribs celery, chopped
1 scallion, minced
1/2 to 1 cup mayonnaise

1 cup sliced seedless red or green grapes
1/2 cup sliced almonds, lightly toasted
Salt and pepper to taste

Combine the chicken, celery, scallion and mayonnaise in a bowl and mix well. Fold in the grapes and almonds. Season with salt and pepper. You may prepare the salad 1 day in advance. Store, covered, in the refrigerator. If preparing in advance, do not add the almonds until just before serving.

Yield: 6 servings

POACHED CHICKEN

The secret to a tasy chicken breast is to purchase chicken breasts with the bone in and skin on to prevent drying out while cooking. To poach, combine 3 chicken breasts with 1 rib celery, halved, 1 unpeeled carrot, halved, 1 sprig fresh parsley and a dash of salt with water to cover in a medium saucepan. Bring to a boil over high heat. Reduce the heat to medium and cook for 10 minutes. Remove from the heat. Let stand until cool before removing the skin.

THAI PORK SALAD

We enjoy this salad as a light summer supper or as an unexpected appetizer. The pork filling may be made several hours ahead and stored in the refrigerator.

2/3 cup fresh lime juice
1/2 cup soy sauce
1 tablespoon sugar
2 teaspoons Thai roasted chili paste
1/3 cup chicken broth
11/2 pounds ground pork
1 cup thinly sliced scallions
3 tablespoons minced fresh lemongrass (optional)
1 tablespoon chopped seeded fresh jalapeño chile
1/2 cup chopped fresh cilantro leaves
1/3 cup chopped fresh mint leaves
Salt and pepper to taste
2 small heads Boston lettuce or endive, leaves separated

Combine the lime juice, soy sauce, sugar and chili paste in a small bowl and mix well and set aside. Bring the chicken broth to a simmer in a sauté pan over medium heat. Add the pork and cook for 8 minutes or until brown and crumbly, stirring frequently. Add the scallions, lemongrass and jalapeño chile and mix well. Cook for 4 minutes or until the green onions are tender and the liquid is absorbed, stirring occasionally. Remove from the heat.

Stir in the lime mixture and the cilantro and mint. Season with salt and pepper. To serve, spoon the mixture onto each lettuce leaf.

Yield: 4 servings

BEST BALSAMIC VINAIGRETTE

The name says it all!

3 tablespoons olive oil
2 tablespoons balsamic vinegar
1 tablespoon Dijon mustard

1 tablespoon honey
Pinch of salt
Pinch of pepper

Combine the olive oil, vinegar, mustard, honey, salt and pepper in a jar with a tight-fitting lid and shake to blend. Toss with salad greens, blue cheese, dried cherries or cranberries and toasted walnuts. This will keep in the refrigerator for up to 1 week.

Yield: 1 cup

LEMON DIJON VINAIGRETTE

This classic dressing pairs well with the Greek Shrimp Sauté on page 74. You may also create a delicious entrée salad by tossing field greens, croutons, Parmesan cheese and the dressing together and then topping with sliced grilled chicken breasts.

2 tablespoons fresh lemon juice
1 teaspoon Dijon mustard
Pinch of sea salt
1/4 teaspoon freshly ground pepper
1 fresh garlic clove, crushed
6 tablespoons extra-virgin olive oil

Combine the lemon juice, mustard, sea salt, pepper and garlic in a small bowl and mix well. Add the olive oil gradually, whisking constantly until blended. Chill, covered, for several hours before serving to allow the flavors to blend. This will keep in the refrigerator for up to 3 days. To use as a marinade, you may double the recipe and add 1/4 cup chopped fresh herbs of your choice, such as parsley, basil, rosemary or thyme.

Yield: 1/2 cup

CROUTONS

There is nothing better than crispy homemade croutons.

3 tablespoons unsalted butter
3 tablespoons olive oil
3 cups day-old bread, cut into 1/2-inch cubes
2 fresh garlic cloves, minced (optional)
Salt to taste

Heat the butter and olive oil in a large skillet over medium-high heat. Add the bread cubes and cook for 3 to 4 minutes or just until the bread begins to brown, tossing constantly with a wooden spoon. Add the garlic and cook until the bread is golden brown. Sprinkle with salt and toss gently. Remove from the heat and let stand until cool. The croutons may be kept in an airtight container until ready to use. You may change the flavor of the croutons by adding a teaspoon of dried mixed herbs, Parmesan cheese or ground red pepper to taste.

Yield: 3 cups

ICED LEMONADE WITH VODKA AND MINT

A cool, refreshing beverage on a hot summer evening!

1 1/3 cups sugar
1 cup packed fresh mint, stemmed
2 lemons, sliced
2 cups freshly squeezed lemon juice (about 10 lemons)

2 cups good quality vodka
1/2 cup water
Ice cubes
1 liter club soda
Lemon slices
Mint sprigs

Combine the sugar, mint and lemons in a pitcher and mash lightly with the back of a wooden spoon. Let stand for 30 minutes. Add the lemon juice, vodka and water and stir until the sugar is dissolved. Chill for 30 minutes to 2 hours. Strain the lemonade and discard the mint. To serve, fill a tall glass or goblet with ice. Pour the lemonade to fill 1/3 of the glass and top with the club soda. Stir to blend. Garnish with a lemon slice and a mint sprig.

Yield: 8 servings

PINK GRAPEFRUIT MARGARITA

This margarita is a Tampa favorite! You can make it ahead and chill until ready to serve.

1¹/₃ cups pink grapefruit juice
²/₃ cup tequila
¹/₄ cup Grand Marnier
Juice of 1 lime

¹/₃ cup sugar or to taste
Crushed ice
Lime slices or grapefruit slices
Coarse salt (optional)

Combine the grapefruit juice, tequila, Grand Marnier, lime juice and sugar in a pitcher and stir until the sugar is dissolved. Add crushed ice to fill the pitcher. Strain the margarita into the prepared glass and garnish with a slice of lime or pink grapefruit. Process the mixture with ice in a blender for a frozen drink. You may moisten the rim of the glass and dip in the salt before filling with the margarita if desired.

Yield: 4 to 6 servings

RED ROCKETS

This recipe is two drinks in one! Serve over ice as a light, refreshing beverage—perfect for a summer get-together—or straight up in martini glasses for a sophisticated cocktail.

2 cups cranberry juice
1 cup fresh orange juice
1 cup orange-flavored or
regular vodka

¹/₄ cup lime juice
Fresh cranberries
Orange slices or lime slices

Combine the cranberry juice, orange juice, vodka and lime juice in a pitcher and mix well. To serve on the rocks, refrigerate until very cold and serve over ice. To serve frozen, freeze in a plastic container for 2 to 3 hours or until slushy and serve in martini glasses. Garnish with skewers of cranberries and orange or lime slices.

Yield: 4 servings

APPLE GINGER FIZZ

This non-alcoholic beverage is perfect for toasting all special occasions.
The ginger adds an unexpected zing!

1/2 cup water
1/2 cup sugar
4 ounces fresh gingerroot, peeled and cut into 1/2-inch slices
1 (750 ml) bottle sparkling apple cider

Combine the water and sugar in a small heavy saucepan over medium-high heat. Add the gingerroot and bring to a boil. Cook for 2 minutes, stirring occasionally. Remove from the heat and let stand, covered, until cool. Strain the syrup and discard the gingerroot. To serve, pour 1 to 2 teaspoons of the syrup into a champagne flute or wine glass. Top with the sparkling cider. You may store the syrup in the refrigerator for up to 1 week.

Yield: 6 to 8 servings

HOT CHOCOLATE

Your children will love this hot chocolate so much, they will want to make it themselves!

1/2 cup whipping cream
1 tablespoon confectioners' sugar
3 cups milk
1 1/2 cups (6 ounces) grated
semisweet chocolate
1/2 teaspoon vanilla extract

Pinch of salt
Chocolate shavings (optional)
Crushed peppermint
candy (optional)
Toffee pieces (optional)

Combine the whipping cream and confectioners' sugar in a small mixing bowl and beat until soft peaks form. Chill, covered, in the refrigerator. You may whip the cream several hours in advance and keep chilled until ready to use. Heat the milk in a heavy saucepan over low heat until warm, being careful not to boil. Add the grated chocolate and stir until melted. Stir in the vanilla and salt. Pour into mugs. Top with a dollop of whipped cream and chocolate shavings, crushed peppermint candy or toffee pieces.

Yield: 4 servings

SIDES & BREADS

MACARONI AND CHEESE WITH BLACK FOREST HAM

*All the comfort of the traditional macaroni and cheese with
a twist of roasted garlic and thyme.*

1¹/2 tablespoons garlic oil
(see page 49)
2 large shallots, minced
2 cups milk
2 cups heavy cream
1/2 teaspoon chopped
fresh thyme
1/8 teaspoon finely grated
lemon zest
10 roasted garlic cloves
(see page 49), mashed
1/2 cup grated Parmesan cheese

8 ounces (2 cups) shredded
extra-sharp Cheddar cheese
8 ounces (2 cups) cubed Black
Forest ham
1 pound bowtie or elbow pasta,
cooked al dente
1 cup fresh bread crumbs
1/2 cup finely grated Parmesan
cheese
3 tablespoons garlic oil
(see page 49)
1 tablespoon chopped fresh parsley

Heat 1¹/2 tablespoons garlic oil in a large saucepan over medium heat. Add the shallots and sauté for 4 minutes or until tender. Whisk in the milk, cream, thyme, lemon zest and garlic. Simmer over medium heat for 30 minutes or until reduced to 2³/4 cups, stirring occasionally. Reduce the heat to low. Add 1/2 cup Parmesan cheese and the Cheddar cheese gradually, stirring until blended. Add the ham and mix well. Add the pasta and toss to combine. Spoon the mixture into a 9×13-inch baking pan sprayed with nonstick cooking spray.

Preheat the oven to 350 degrees. Combine the bread crumbs, 1/2 cup Parmesan cheese and 3 tablespoons garlic oil in a bowl and mix well. Sprinkle over the prepared dish. Bake for 20 to 30 minutes or until the mixture is bubbly and the bread crumbs are golden brown. Sprinkle with the parsley and serve immediately.

Ask for Black Forest ham at the deli counter to be cut into 1-inch slices. Cut into cubes at home.

Yield: 6 servings

OVEN-ROASTED ASPARAGUS WITH THYME-SHALLOT VINAIGRETTE

1 large bunch asparagus, trimmed
1 tablespoon extra-virgin olive oil
1 fresh garlic clove, thinly sliced
3 tablespoons shredded fresh Parmesan cheese
1 tablespoon red wine vinegar

1 tablespoon extra-virgin olive oil
1/2 teaspoon Dijon mustard
1 to 2 tablespoons minced shallots
1/2 teaspoon stemmed and minced fresh thyme
Salt and freshly ground pepper to taste

Preheat the oven to 400 degrees. Place the asparagus in a large roasting pan. Add 1 tablespoon olive oil and the garlic and toss to coat. Roast for 12 to 20 minutes or until tender-crisp, stirring once. Top with the Parmesan cheese and bake for 2 to 3 minutes or until the cheese is melted.

Whisk together the vinegar, 1 tablespoon olive oil, mustard, shallots and thyme in a small bowl. Season with salt and pepper. Arrange the asparagus on a large serving platter. Pour the olive oil mixture evenly over the asparagus and toss gently to coat. Serve immediately.

Yield: 4 servings

ROASTED GARLIC

To roast garlic, place 3/4 cup (about 2 heads) fresh peeled garlic cloves in a small baking dish. Pour 1 cup olive oil over the garlic. Bake, covered with foil, at 350 degrees for 40 minutes or until golden brown. Remove from the oven and let stand until cool. Strain the garlic, reserving the garlic and the oil. The oil may be used as a substitute for olive oil or butter. The oil may be stored in the refrigerator for up to 1 week. Yield: 3/4 cup.

FRESH CARROT SALAD

Sometimes the simplest of ingredients yield the most delicious results. A light Dijon vinaigrette highlights the flavors and textures of crunchy carrots and toasted almonds.

3 tablespoons white wine vinegar
1 teaspoon Dijon mustard
1/2 teaspoon salt
1/2 cup olive oil
2 pounds carrots, grated
1/2 cup slivered almonds, toasted

Combine the vinegar, mustard and salt in a small bowl and whisk until blended. Whisk in the olive oil and set aside. Combine the vinaigrette with the carrots in a large bowl and toss to mix well. Spoon into a serving dish. Sprinkle with the almonds when ready to serve.

Yield: 6 to 8 servings

SWEET CORN AND PEPPER SALAD

Farm-fresh corn, peppers, and a cilantro-lime vinaigrette create a colorful salad to enjoy with the Cuban Wrap (page 88) or as a topping for grilled seafood.

6 ears of corn, or 4 1/2 cups frozen corn
1/4 to 1/2 cup water
1 yellow bell pepper, seeded and chopped
1 red bell pepper, seeded and chopped
1 small red onion, minced
(about 1/2 cup)

1/2 cup fresh cilantro, stemmed and
chopped
1/4 cup fresh lime juice
1/4 cup olive oil
Salt and pepper to taste

Cut the corn off the cobs. Combine with the water in a medium saucepan. Cook, covered, over medium heat for 5 minutes or just until tender; drain. Let stand until cool. Combine with the yellow pepper, red pepper, onion, cilantro, lime juice, olive oil and salt and pepper in a large bowl and mix well. Chill, covered, for several hours. Garnish with additional cilantro if desired. You may prepare the salad 1 day in advance.

Yield: 6 to 8 servings

GARLIC GREEN BEANS

Fresh garlic and parsley accent green beans in this side dish. Pair it with the Roasted Salmon with Tomato Cream Sauce (page 81) for a weeknight dinner so good you'll swear you're in a restaurant.

1 pound fresh green beans
4 fresh garlic cloves, crushed
1/8 teaspoon salt
1/8 teaspoon pepper

3 tablespoons butter
1/3 cup stemmed and chopped
fresh parsley

Snap the ends from the green beans. Bring 6 quarts water to a boil in a large saucepan over high heat. Add the green beans and reduce the heat to medium. Boil for 7 minutes; drain and set aside. Sauté the garlic, salt and pepper in the butter in a large skillet over medium heat until the garlic is softened. Add the beans and cook for 3 minutes, stirring occasionally. Stir in the parsley and serve immediately.

Yield: 8 servings

BROCCOLI WITH GOAT CHEESE

This unusual pairing of creamy goat cheese with tender broccoli will soon be a family favorite. This dish may also be used as a topping for pasta.

2 stalks broccoli
1 teaspoon salt
4 to 5 ounces creamy goat
cheese, chopped

1/4 cup (1/2 stick) unsalted
butter, chopped
Salt and pepper to taste

Trim the broccoli florets from the stalks. Slice off the outside of the broccoli stalks to reveal the tender green interior using a vegetable peeler. Slice the stalks into 1/2-inch circles.

Fill a sauté pan with 1/2 inch of water and add 1 teaspoon salt. Arrange the broccoli in a single layer in the sauté pan. Bring to a slow boil and cook, covered, for 3 to 5 minutes or until tender-crisp; drain. Reduce the heat to low. Add the cheese and butter and stir until the cheese is melted. Season with salt and pepper. You may substitute 6 cups broccoli florets for the 2 stalks broccoli if desired.

Yield: 6 servings

EGGPLANT PROVOLONE STACK

*If your time is limited, substitute 2 large onions, thinly sliced and sautéed in
2 tablespoons olive oil, for the Slow-Cooked Onions.*

1 eggplant	8 ounces provolone cheese,
Salt to taste	sliced
3 to 4 large tomatoes	Freshly ground pepper to taste
1 cup Slow-Cooked Onions	Basil chiffonade (see page 37)
(see below)	

Cut the eggplant horizontally into 1/8-inch slices. Arrange a single layer of the eggplant slices over
the bottom of a large bowl. Sprinkle with salt. Repeat the process until all the eggplant is used. Place
a plate with a weight on top of the eggplant and let stand for 30 minutes. Preheat the oven to 350 degrees.
Cut the tomatoes into 1/4-inch slices. Rinse the eggplant and pat dry. Arrange the eggplant on a baking
sheet. Top each eggplant slice with 1 to 2 heaping tablespoons of the onions, a tomato slice and
a cheese slice. Bake for 15 to 20 minutes or until the cheese is melted and golden brown. Remove from
the oven and season with salt and pepper. Garnish with basil chiffonade.

Yield: 4 main-dish servings or 6 to 8 appetizer servings

SLOW-COOKED ONIONS

Combine 5 pounds sliced Vidalia onions, 1/2 cup butter

and 1/4 cup port in a slow cooker. Cook on High for 12 to 14 hours

or until the onions are dark brown. Store in the refrigerator for up

to 1 week. Skim the butter off the top before using if desired.

Unlike caramelized onions cooked over the stove, these have a lot of

juice. If a recipe requires less liquid, strain and use the liquid in

sauces or to flavor soups. These make a wonderful topping for

grilled chicken breasts or homemade pizza. Yield: 6 cups.

CHERRY TOMATOES PROVENÇAL

Cherry tomatoes are elevated to elegance with this herbed topping. This can easily be made ahead and set aside until you are ready to roast.

1 pint cherry tomatoes, stemmed
1/2 cup bread crumbs
1/4 cup minced onion
1 fresh garlic clove, minced
1/4 cup stemmed and chopped
fresh parsley

1/4 teaspoon crumbled thyme
1/2 teaspoon salt
Dash of pepper
1/4 cup olive oil

Preheat the oven to 425 degrees. Arrange the tomatoes in a single layer in a lightly oiled shallow baking dish. Combine the bread crumbs, onion, garlic, parsley, thyme, salt, pepper and olive oil in a bowl and mix well. Sprinkle over the tomatoes. Roast for 10 to 15 minutes or until the tomatoes are tender.

Yield: 4 servings

ZUCCHINI SAUTÉ

Believe it or not, your kids will even like this! Shred the zucchini, and let it sit while you prepare the rest of the meal. Sauté just before serving.

4 zucchini, coarsely grated
2 tablespoons kosher salt
2 tablespoons olive oil
1 fresh garlic clove, finely
chopped

Pepper to taste
2 tablespoons freshly grated
Parmesan cheese

Place the zucchini in a colander and sprinkle with the kosher salt. Let sit for 10 minutes to 1 hour; rinse. Squeeze the excess water from the zucchini. Heat the olive oil in a medium sauté pan over medium-high heat. Add the garlic and cook until softened. Add the zucchini and cook for 3 to 5 minutes, stirring occasionally. Season with pepper. Spoon into a serving dish and sprinkle with the Parmesan cheese.

Yield: 4 to 6 servings

CREAMY POLENTA

This creamy polenta will vie with mashed potatoes for the ultimate comfort food.
Substitute it when you would usually serve rice, potatoes, or pasta for a new taste treat.
Polenta may also be poured into a loaf pan or pie pan and chilled, then sliced
and pan-fried for a tasty alternative.

5 cups milk
1 cup medium-grain yellow cornmeal (do not use instant)
1 teaspoon kosher salt
1/4 teaspoon white pepper

Bring the milk slowly to a boil in a medium saucepan over medium heat, stirring frequently with a wooden spoon. Gradually add the cornmeal, whisking constantly. Reduce the heat to low and cook for 20 to 40 minutes or until the mixture is thick and smooth, stirring frequently with a wooden spoon to prevent lumps. Do not let the mixture come to a bubbling boil. Season with the kosher salt and white pepper. Spoon into a serving dish and serve warm. You may stir in 8 ounces mascarpone cheese or 1 cup fontina cheese just before serving if desired.

Yield: 8 servings

FRESH MANGO CARROT CHUTNEY

Coarsely shred 3 green mangoes and 1 large carrot. Combine
with 1 tablespoon peeled and minced fresh gingerroot, 1 fresh garlic
clove, minced, 1/2 cup rice wine vinegar, 3 tablespoons molasses,
1 tablespoon crushed coriander seeds and the juice of 1 lime in a
bowl and mix well. Chill, covered, for 1 hour or longer to allow the
flavors to blend before serving. Serve with Crispy Duck
Breasts (page 95). Yield: about 2 1/2 cups.

WILD RICE WITH CRANBERRIES AND ALMONDS

*This easy rice dish is an elegant addition to any fall or
winter meal and may be made ahead.*

1/2 cup wild rice
1 cup chicken broth
1/2 cup brown rice
1 cup chicken broth
3 tablespoons butter
3 onions, thinly sliced
1 tablespoon light brown sugar
1 cup dried cranberries
1 tablespoon grated orange zest
1/4 cup sliced almonds, toasted
1/4 cup stemmed and chopped fresh parsley

Cook the wild rice using the package directions, substituting 1 cup chicken broth for the water. Cook the brown rice using the package directions, substituting 1 cup chicken broth for the water. Melt the butter in a sauté pan over medium low heat. Add the onions and brown sugar and cook for 25 minutes, stirring frequently. Add the cranberries and cook for 10 minutes or until the cranberries are plump, stirring frequently. Stir in the orange zest. Combine with the wild rice, brown rice and almonds in a large bowl and mix well. Spoon into a serving dish and garnish with the parsley. Serve warm or at room temperature.

Yield: 6 to 8 servings

LEMON RICE

This savory rice goes well with grilled meat or fish.

1 cup white or basmati rice
1/4 cup (1/2 stick) butter
1 teaspoon salt
1 teaspoon mustard seeds

1 teaspoon turmeric
Juice of 1 lemon
   (about 2 tablespoons),
   strained

Cook the rice using the package directions. Melt the butter in a small saucepan over medium heat. Add the salt, mustard seeds and turmeric and cook until the mustard seeds "dance," stirring constantly. Combine with the rice and lemon juice in a serving bowl and mix well. Serve immediately.

Yield: 2 to 4 servings

SAFFRON RISOTTO

4 cups chicken broth
2 tablespoons unsalted butter
1 shallot, finely chopped
1 cup arborio rice

1/2 cup white wine
Saffron threads, crumbled
1 cup grated Parmesan cheese
Salt and pepper to taste

Bring the chicken broth to a boil in a small saucepan over high heat. Reduce the temperature to low. Melt the butter in a heavy saucepan over medium heat. Add the shallot and sauté until the shallot is translucent. Add the rice and cook until the rice begins to appear translucent, stirring constantly. Add the wine and cook for 2 minutes or until the liquid is absorbed. Add 1/2 cup of the broth and cook until most of the liquid is absorbed, stirring constantly. Continue adding the broth, 1/2 cup at a time, cooking and stirring until most of the liquid is absorbed before adding additional broth. Add the saffron and mix well. Remove from the heat. The mixture will be creamy. Stir in the Parmesan cheese and salt and pepper and serve immediately.

Yield: 2 1/2 cups

PENNE WITH WILD MUSHROOMS AND ASPARAGUS

A tasty dish that makes an elegant side dish or a great vegetarian dinner. You may also add chicken for a quick one-dish dinner.

2 cups penne pasta
2 tablespoons unsalted butter
4 teaspoons olive oil
4 ounces wild mushrooms, sliced
2 tablespoons chopped shallots
2 fresh garlic cloves, minced
2 tablespoons chicken broth
1/4 cup madeira or marsala

2 tablespoons stemmed and chopped
   fresh parsley
2 tablespoons stemmed and coarsely
   chopped fresh tarragon or fresh basil
4 teaspoons freshly grated Parmesan cheese
6 asparagus spears, blanched and cut into
   3/4-inch pieces
Salt and pepper to taste

Cook the pasta using the package directions; drain, reserving 1/4 cup of the liquid. Heat the butter and olive oil in a medium saucepan over medium-high heat. Add the mushrooms and sauté for 1 to 2 minutes. Reduce the heat to medium. Add the shallots and garlic and cook for 2 minutes or until the shallots soften, stirring frequently. Add the chicken broth and cook until most of the liquid is evaporated. Add the wine and cook for 2 minutes. Add the pasta, reserved liquid, parsley, tarragon, Parmesan cheese and asparagus and mix well. Let cook until heated through. Season with salt and pepper.

Yield: 4 side-dish servings or 2 main-dish servings

BLANCHING VEGETABLES

To blanch a vegetable means to boil it briefly, retaining the color

and crunchy texture. To prepare the asparagus in the recipe,

cook the asparagus in a pot of rapidly boiling salted water

for 2 to 4 minutes. Immediately plunge the asparagus in ice

water to stop the cooking process; drain.

TOMATO BASIL SAUCE

This thick, rich marinara sauce has been a family tradition for generations. Use it as a base for a sensational pasta dish or as a sauce for homemade pizza.

1/4 cup olive oil
1 large Spanish onion,
  finely chopped
4 large fresh garlic cloves, minced
2 (28-ounce) cans crushed
  tomatoes
1 (6-ounce) can tomato purée

1/2 cup stemmed and finely chopped
  fresh basil
1/4 cup stemmed and finely chopped
  fresh oregano
1/2 teaspoon salt
1/2 teaspoon black pepper
1/4 teaspoon red pepper

Heat the olive oil in a large saucepan over medium-high heat. Add the onions and garlic and cook until the onions are translucent, stirring frequently. Do not let the garlic burn. Add the crushed tomatoes and tomato purée and mix well. Reduce the heat to medium and cook, covered, for 30 minutes, skimming the sauce frequently. Stir in the basil, oregano, salt, black pepper and red pepper. Reduce the heat to low and cook, covered, for 2 to 3 hours or until the sauce has thickened and the flavors are incorporated. Season with additional salt to taste. Serve over your favorite pasta.

Yield: 4 servings

There are many wines that are good, safe bets and are flexible with many types of food. When planning a dinner party or ordering at a restaurant, consider these wines. In the white variety, try sauvignon blanc, pinot blanc, pinot grigio, Australian riesling, and unoaked chardonnay. If you're looking for a food-friendly red wine, a merlot, pinot noir, Spanish red, or an Australian shiraz would be a good choice.

DOUBLE APPLE MUFFINS

Chopped apples and applesauce team up to give these muffins great texture and moisture. These are fast to put together and freeze well for a quick breakfast or snack.

BROWN SUGAR TOPPING
1/3 cup flour
1/3 cup firmly packed brown sugar
1/2 teaspoon cinnamon
3 tablespoons butter, chilled and chopped

MUFFINS

2 cups flour	1/4 cup (1/2 stick) unsalted butter,
1 1/2 teaspoons baking powder	melted
1/2 teaspoon baking soda	1/3 cup sugar
1/2 teaspoon salt	1/3 cup firmly packed brown sugar
1 teaspoon cinnamon	1 egg, beaten
1/2 teaspoon ground cloves	1 cup applesauce
1/4 cup vegetable oil	1 cup chopped peeled apple

For the topping, combine the flour, brown sugar and cinnamon in a bowl. Cut in the butter with a pastry blender or 2 knives until crumbly.

For the muffins, preheat the oven to 400 degrees. Grease 12 muffin cups. Combine the flour, baking powder, baking soda, salt, cinnamon and cloves in a large bowl. Combine the oil, butter, sugar, brown sugar, egg and applesauce in a medium bowl and mix well. Add to the dry ingredients and stir just until combined. Fold in the apple. Fill the prepared muffin cups. Sprinkle with the topping, gently pressing the topping into the batter. Bake for 15 to 17 minutes or until the topping is golden brown and a wooden pick inserted in the center of a muffin comes out clean.

Yield: 12 muffins

ROSEMARY PARMESAN MUFFINS

Regular or mini-sized, these muffins are a welcome change from the usual bread or rolls.
Try these with Roasted Vegetable Soup (page 38) or the Tuscan Frittata (page 89).

3 cups flour	1 cup shredded Parmesan cheese
1 tablespoon baking powder	10 tablespoons unsalted butter,
1/2 teaspoon baking soda	melted
1/2 teaspoon salt	2 eggs
2 tablespoons stemmed and	1 cup sour cream
chopped fresh rosemary	

Preheat the oven to 375 degrees. Combine the flour, baking powder, baking soda and salt in a large bowl. Add the rosemary and Parmesan cheese; mix well and set aside. Combine the butter, eggs and sour cream in a medium bowl and mix well. Add to the dry ingredients and stir just until combined; the batter will be the consistency of biscuit dough.

Spoon the mixture into 12 to 14 greased muffin cups or 36 greased mini muffin cups, filling them 2/3 full. Bake for 15 minutes for the regular muffins or for 8 to 10 minutes for the mini muffins or until golden brown. Remove to a wire rack. We recommend that these muffins be served warm.

Yield: 12 to 14 regular muffins or 36 mini muffins

MUFFIN VARIATIONS

For Cheddar Bacon Muffins, substitute 1/2 cup chopped cooked bacon and 1 cup shredded sharp Cheddar cheese for the rosemary and Parmesan cheese. For Thyme Caramelized Onion Muffins, substitute 1 cup chopped caramelized onion and 1 1/2 tablespoons fresh thyme for the rosemary and Parmesan cheese.

BLUEBERRY BANANA BREAKFAST BREAD

This moist coffee cake is perfect for morning meetings or packed for a school snack. The topping ingredients may be doubled if you like it "bakery style."

PECAN TOPPING
1/4 cup flour
2 tablespoons sugar
1/4 teaspoon cinnamon
1/4 cup chopped pecans
2 tablespoons chilled butter, chopped

BREAD

2 cups flour	1 cup sugar
1 tablespoon baking powder	1 egg
1/2 teaspoon cinnamon	1 cup mashed bananas
1/2 teaspoon salt	(3 to 4 bananas)
1/4 cup (1/2 stick) butter,	1/2 cup milk
softened	2 cups fresh blueberries

For the topping, combine the flour, sugar, cinnamon and pecans in a bowl. Cut in the butter with a pastry blender, 2 knives or with your fingers until crumbly and set aside.

For the bread, preheat the oven to 350 degrees. Butter an 8×8-inch baking dish or a round 2-quart baking dish. Combine the flour, baking powder, cinnamon and salt in a small bowl and set aside. Cream the butter and sugar in a small mixing bowl until light and fluffy. Add the egg and beat until blended. Combine the banana and milk in a bowl and mix well. Add to the creamed mixture alternately with the dry ingredients, mixing well after each addition. Fold in the blueberries.

Pour into the prepared baking dish. Sprinkle with the topping. Bake for 1 hour or until a wooden pick inserted in the center comes out clean.

Yield: 8 to 10 servings

CARROT BREAD

A quick bread for breakfast on the go or packed as a mid-morning snack.
Your children won't even know they are eating vegetables!

1¹/3 cups flour
1¹/3 cups sugar
1¹/4 teaspoons cinnamon
1¹/4 teaspoons baking soda
¹/2 teaspoon salt
3 eggs, beaten
2 cups shredded carrots
²/3 cup vegetable oil
¹/2 cup chopped pecans (optional)

Preheat the oven to 375 degrees. Sift together the flour, sugar, cinnamon, baking soda and salt into a bowl. Add the eggs and mix well. Add the carrots and oil and mix well. Stir in the pecans. Pour into a greased and floured 5×9-inch loaf pan. Bake for 1 hour. Remove to a wire rack to cool.

This bread keeps well in the refrigerator or freezer. You may use mini loaf pans, decreasing the baking time to 35 minutes, if desired.

Yield: one 9-inch loaf

"My kitchen is a mystical place, a kind of temple for
me. It is a place where the surfaces seem to have significance,
where the sounds and odors carry meaning that transfers
from the past and bridges to the future."
—*Pearl Bailey*

CINNAMON STREUSEL COFFEE CAKE

*Testers loved this cake for its great taste and ease of preparation. It makes three 8-inch cakes,
which are great to take to meetings, give to a neighbor, or freeze to be enjoyed later.*

3 cups flour
1 cup sugar
1 cup packed brown sugar
1 1/2 teaspoons cinnamon
1/2 cup chopped pecans
1 cup (2 sticks) unsalted butter, softened
1 teaspoon baking powder
1 teaspoon baking soda
1/2 teaspoon salt
1 cup buttermilk
2 eggs
1 teaspoon vanilla extract

Preheat the oven to 350 degrees. Combine the flour, sugar, brown sugar, cinnamon and pecans in a bowl. Cut in the butter with a pastry blender or your fingers until crumbly. Reserve 1 cup of the mixture. Combine the remaining mixture with the baking powder, baking soda and salt and mix well. Combine the buttermilk, eggs and vanilla in a small bowl and mix well. Add to the dry ingredients and mix gently. The batter will be slightly lumpy.

Pour the batter evenly into 3 greased and floured 8-inch cake or springform pans. Sprinkle the reserved crumb mixture evenly over the batter. Bake for 20 to 25 minutes or until the edges begin to pull away from the sides of the pans and a cake tester inserted in the center comes out with a moist crumb. Remove to wire racks to cool.

Yield: three 8-inch cakes

POPOVERS

What fun you and your children will have making this batter and watching it miraculously puff up and turn golden brown! The crisp shell and soft interior make a great partner for our Italian Sausage Soup with Tortellini (page 35) or with butter and confectioners' sugar for a sweet treat.

2 eggs
3/4 cup milk
1/4 cup water
1 tablespoon butter, melted
1 cup flour
1/2 teaspoon salt

Preheat the oven to 375 degrees. Heat a 12-cup muffin pan or popover pan in the oven for 10 minutes. Combine the eggs, milk, water and butter in a medium bowl and whisk until blended. Combine the flour and salt in a small bowl. Add to the egg mixture and whisk just until combined.

Remove the pan from the oven and brush the muffin cups with vegetable oil. Pour the batter into the prepared muffin cups, filling 3/4 full. Bake for 30 minutes. Do not open the oven door. Popovers will be puffed and golden brown. Remove from the oven and serve immediately.

For Garlic-Thyme Popovers, sauté 1 minced fresh garlic clove and 1 tablespoon chopped fresh thyme in 1 tablespoon butter. Substitute the mixture for the butter and prepare as directed above.

Yield: 12 popovers

PUFFY BREAKFAST CAKES

*This recipe can easily be doubled or tripled to feed a crowd. You can also bake it
in one large pan rather than ramekins.*

2 eggs
1/3 cup milk
2 tablespoons orange juice
1/3 cup flour
3 tablespoons sugar
Pinch of salt
4 tablespoons (1/2 stick) unsalted butter

Preheat the oven to 425 degrees. Combine the eggs, milk, orange juice, flour, sugar and salt in
a mixing bowl and beat until blended. Place 1 tablespoon butter in each of four 1-cup ramekins. Place
in the oven and heat until the butter sizzles. Remove from the oven and pour the batter evenly into the
ramekins. Bake for 20 minutes or until puffed and golden. Serve immediately with syrup or Strawberry
Sauce (below) and sour cream.

Yield: 4 cakes

STRAWBERRY SAUCE

Crush 1 quart fresh strawberries. Combine with 1/4 cup sugar and

mix well, or combine 1 (10-ounce) package frozen strawberries with

1 tablespoon orange juice in a small saucepan over medium heat and

cook until heated through, stirring occasionally.

BUTTERMILK CORN CAKES

This makes a savory pancake alternative for supper. Serve with ham, roast pork, or other grilled meats. You can also add 2 tablespoons chopped chives to the batter and serve with sour cream.

1¹/4 cups cornmeal
¹/4 cup flour
¹/2 teaspoon baking soda
¹/2 teaspoon salt
¹/2 teaspoon pepper
1³/4 cups buttermilk
2 eggs, lightly beaten
3 tablespoons vegetable oil
1¹/2 cups frozen corn, thawed

Combine the cornmeal, flour, baking soda, salt and pepper in a large bowl and set aside. Whisk together the buttermilk, eggs and oil in a small bowl. Add to the dry ingredients and stir just until combined. Stir in the corn.

Pour a small amount of batter onto a hot, lightly greased skillet or griddle. Cook over medium-high heat until bubbles appear on the surface and the underside is golden brown. Turn the pancake and cook until golden brown. Keep warm in the oven until ready to serve. Serve warm.

Yield: 24 corn cakes

BASIC HERB BUTTER

Combine ¹/2 cup (1 stick) softened unsalted butter, 1 to 3 tablespoons
dried herbs or 2 to 6 tablespoons minced fresh herbs of your choice,
¹/2 teaspoon lemon juice and white pepper to taste in a small
bowl and mix well. Let stand for 1 hour or longer to allow the
flavors to blend before using. Yield: ¹/2 cup.

SATURDAY MORNING PANCAKES

Making pancakes is a cherished ritual in many homes. You may enjoy the leisurely pace of a weekend morning a little more by doing some preparation the night before. Mix the liquid and dry ingredients separately, and refrigerate the liquid ingredients overnight. Combine in the morning while the griddle or skillet is heating.

2 cups flour
3 teaspoons baking powder
1/2 teaspoon salt
3 tablespoons sugar
2 eggs, lightly beaten
2 cups milk
1/2 cup vegetable oil

Sift together the flour, baking powder, salt and sugar into a large bowl. Whisk together the eggs, milk and oil in a small bowl. Add to the dry ingredients and whisk until blended. Let stand for 30 minutes.

Heat a large nonstick skillet or griddle over medium to medium-high heat. Brush the skillet with vegetable oil. Pour 1/4 cup of the batter onto the prepared skillet. Cook for 2 to 3 minutes or until bubbles appear on the surface and the underside is golden brown. Turn the pancake and cook until golden brown. Repeat the process with the remaining batter, brushing the skillet with oil before adding the batter. You may substitute 1 cup whole wheat flour for 1 cup flour if desired.

Yield: 20 pancakes

POTATO PANCAKES

Our kid tasters asked for seconds of these crispy potatoes. For a quick side dish or breakfast accompaniment, these can be frozen and reheated in a 350-degree oven until hot.

3 large potatoes, peeled and shredded
1 onion, grated
2 eggs, beaten
2 tablespoons flour
1 teaspoon salt
1/4 teaspoon pepper
1/2 to 3/4 cup vegetable oil

Combine the potatoes and onion in a large bowl. Add the eggs, flour, salt and pepper and mix well. Let stand for 15 minutes. The potatoes may darken. Heat the oil in a large sauté pan over medium-high heat. Squeeze the additional liquid from 1/4 cup of the mixture and form the mixture into a ball. Place in the prepared pan. Flatten with the back of a fork into a 2- to 3-inch disk. Cook for 2 to 3 minutes on each side or until golden brown. Remove to a paper towel to drain. Repeat the process until all the potato mixture is used. Keep the cooked pancakes warm in a 150-degree oven. Serve immediately. The potatoes may easily be shredded in the food processor using the grating or shredding blade. They may also be shredded in advance and combined with cold water to cover. Drain well before using.

Yield: 12 to 14 pancakes

PANCAKE VARIATIONS

*For Sweet Potato and Chive Pancakes, substitute
1 large sweet potato, peeled and shredded, for 2 of the white
potatoes, and add 2 tablespoons chopped fresh chives to
the mixture. For Zucchini Potato Pancakes, substitute 1 cup
shredded zucchini for 1 of the potatoes.*

MORNING GRANOLA

*Almonds, toasted oats, and sesame seeds combine to make a healthy and not-too-sweet
cereal. For breakfast, it can be topped with yogurt and berries, or you might
even find yourself sneaking into this all day long!*

5 cups oats (not quick-cooking)
1/3 cup packed dark brown sugar
1/2 cup wheat germ
1/2 cup slivered or sliced almonds
1/4 cup sesame seeds
1/3 cup vegetable oil
1/3 cup light corn syrup
1 teaspoon vanilla extract

Preheat the oven to 350 degrees. Cook the oats in a large baking pan for 20 minutes, stirring
occasionally. Let stand until cool. Combine the oats, brown sugar, wheat germ, almonds and sesame
seeds in a large bowl and mix well. Add the oil, corn syrup and vanilla and stir until the dry ingredients
are coated. Spoon into the baking pan. Bake for 20 to 25 minutes or until browned, stirring often. Let
stand until cool, stirring occasionally. Serve with cold milk, soy milk or yogurt and fruit. Store in an
airtight container or resealable plastic bag. You may add dried cherries, raisins or your choice of nuts
if desired.

Yield: 8 cups

MAIN DISHES

SEAFOOD GUMBO

A big steaming pot of gumbo is wonderful for feeding a crowd. You can make this ahead, and it will keep frozen for up to one month.

1 tablespoon butter
1 cup uncooked rice
2 cups chicken broth
2 tablespoons vegetable oil
2 onions, finely chopped
6 fresh garlic cloves, minced
1/2 tablespoon salt
1/2 tablespoon freshly ground pepper
1 (28-ounce) can crushed tomatoes
1 (28-ounce) can diced tomatoes
7 cups water

1 1/4 pounds fresh or frozen okra, sliced
2 tablespoons Worcestershire sauce
1 1/3 tablespoons filé powder
1 1/2 pounds shrimp, peeled and deveined
1/2 pound backfin crab meat, cleaned
1 pound best quality andouille sausage, cut into 1/4-inch slices
Hot sauce to taste
Salt and pepper to taste

Melt the butter in a medium saucepan over medium heat. Add the rice and stir to coat with the butter. Add the chicken broth and increase the heat to medium-high. Bring to a boil, stirring occasionally. Reduce the heat to low and simmer, covered, for 20 minutes or until the rice is fluffy.

Heat the oil in a large stockpot over medium-low heat. Add the onions, garlic, 1/2 tablespoon salt and 1/2 tablespoon pepper and sauté for 10 minutes or until the onions are tender. Add the crushed tomatoes, undrained diced tomatoes and water and mix well. Add the okra and Worcestershire sauce and bring to a boil. Remove from the heat. Combine the filé powder with 1 to 2 tablespoons water in a small bowl and whisk until blended and thickened. Whisk the filé mixture into the broth until blended.

Add the shrimp, crab meat and sausage and mix well. Cook over medium heat for 15 minutes, stirring occasionally. Add hot sauce and salt and pepper. Serve over the rice or stir the rice into the gumbo before serving.

You may substitute 2 tablespoons Cajun seasoning for the filé powder if desired. Do not mix the Cajun seasoning with water before stirring it into the gumbo.

Yield: 1 gallon

BARBEQUE SHRIMP

Barbeque shrimp is traditionally served with shells and tails left on and accompanied by lots of extra napkins. This recipe is also wonderful made substituting peeled and deveined shrimp with the tails left on. Serve with crusty bread for dipping into the spicy sauce.

1/2 cup (1 stick) butter
2 tablespoons minced fresh garlic
4 bay leaves
1 tablespoon stemmed and chopped fresh rosemary, or
2 teaspoons dried rosemary
1/2 teaspoon dried basil
1/2 teaspoon dried oregano
1 tablespoon paprika
1/2 teaspoon salt

1/2 teaspoon cayenne pepper
3/4 teaspoon freshly ground black pepper
1 tablespoon fresh lemon juice
1 tablespoon Worcestershire sauce
1 cup coarsely chopped celery
2 pounds large unpeeled shrimp
6 ounces beer

Melt the butter over medium heat in a heavy ovenproof saucepan. Add the garlic, bay leaves, rosemary, basil, oregano, paprika, salt, cayenne pepper, black pepper, lemon juice, Worcestershire sauce and celery. Reduce the heat to medium-low and simmer for 7 to 8 minutes, stirring frequently. Remove from the heat and let stand for 30 minutes or longer.

Preheat the oven to 450 degrees. Add the shrimp and beer to the saucepan and cook over medium heat until the shrimp turn pink, stirring occasionally. Place the pan in the oven and cook for 10 minutes. Remove the bay leaves. Ladle into individual bowls and serve with French bread.

Yield: 4 servings

GREEK SHRIMP SAUTÉ

A versatile dish that can be served as an appetizer or main course. This favorite shrimp recipe was inspired by the Greek restaurants in nearby Tarpon Springs.

2 pounds large shrimp, peeled, deveined and tails removed	¹/2 cup olive oil
1 tablespoon Lawry's garlic salt	3 tablespoons butter
1 tablespoon dried oregano	1 cup flour
Juice of 1 large lemon	Lemon wedges
	Hot sauce

Combine the shrimp with the garlic salt, oregano and lemon juice in a medium bowl and toss well to coat. Chill, covered, for 45 minutes. Remove the shrimp from the marinade and discard the marinade. Pat the shrimp dry with paper towels. Heat the olive oil and butter in a cast-iron skillet to bubbling but not smoking over medium to medium-high heat. Combine the shrimp with the flour in a large resealable plastic bag and shake to coat. Shake the excess flour off the shrimp and working in batches, place in the skillet, leaving room between each shrimp. Cook until golden brown on all sides and cooked through, turning once. Drain on paper towels. Serve with lemon wedges and hot sauce.

Yield: 4 generous servings

"It seems to me that our three basic needs, for food and security and love, are so mixed and mingled and entwined that we cannot straightly think of one without the others. So it happens that when I write of hunger, I am really writing about love and the hunger for it, and warmth and the love of it and the hunger for it. . . and then the warmth and richness and fine reality of hunger satisfied. . . .and it is all one."
—M.F.K. Fisher

LEMON CAPER SHRIMP WITH ORZO

A quick and delicious one-dish meal that cooks in minutes. Add a green salad and some hot bread for a perfect meal at the end of your busy day.

1¹/2 cups orzo
2 tablespoons olive oil
2 fresh garlic cloves, mashed
1 pound large shrimp, peeled
  with the tails intact
  and deveined
2 tablespoons chopped
  fresh parsley
Salt and freshly ground pepper
  to taste

Juice of 1 lemon
1 cup dry white wine
5 tablespoons unsalted butter
Grated zest of 1 lemon
3 tablespoons capers, drained
2 tablespoons chopped
  fresh parsley
1/2 cup freshly grated
  Parmesan cheese

Cook the orzo using the package directions; drain. Toss with 1 tablespoon olive oil and set aside. Heat the remaining 1 tablespoon olive oil in a large skillet over medium-low heat. Add the garlic and cook for 1 minute, stirring frequently. Add the shrimp, 2 tablespoons parsley, salt and pepper and cook for 2 to 3 minutes, stirring occasionally. Turn the shrimp and cook for 2 minutes or until opaque. Remove the shrimp to a bowl and cover to keep warm.

Add the lemon juice and wine to the skillet and bring to a boil over medium-high heat to deglaze the skillet. Lower the heat to medium-low. Add the butter, lemon zest, capers and shrimp and toss to combine. Cook just until heated through. Spoon the orzo into individual pasta bowls. Spoon the shrimp mixture over the orzo and top with 2 tablespoons parsley and Parmesan cheese.

Yield: 4 servings

GRILLED SCALLOPS IN COCONUT CURRY SAUCE

Grilled scallops are highlighted by the Floridian flavors of citrus and coconut in this sweet and spicy curry dish. Serve the scallops with the sauce on the side for a quick appetizer or over Jasmine rice for a tasty dinner.

SCALLOPS

1 cup orange juice
3 tablespoons finely chopped fresh basil
1 pound sea scallops

COCONUT CURRY SAUCE

1 tablespoon olive oil	1 tablespoon finely chopped
1 tablespoon minced shallots	fresh basil
1 tablespoon curry powder	1/4 teaspoon salt
1 cup unsweetened coconut	1/4 teaspoon dried crushed red pepper
milk	2 teaspoons fresh lime juice

For the scallops, combine the orange juice and basil in a large resealable plastic bag. Add the scallops and turn to coat. Chill in the refrigerator for 45 minutes to 1 hour, turning once. Soak wooden skewers in water for 30 minutes to prevent burning. Remove the scallops and discard the marinade. Thread the scallops onto the skewers and grill over medium to high heat until firm and opaque, turning once.

For the sauce, heat the olive oil in a medium saucepan over medium-high heat. Add the shallots and sauté until softened. Add the curry powder and cook for 1 minute or until the aroma from the curry is released, stirring constantly. Add the coconut milk and bring to a boil. Reduce the heat to medium and add the basil, salt and red pepper and cook for 1 minute, stirring occasionally. Remove from the heat and stir in the lime juice.

Yield: 4 main-dish servings or 8 appetizer servings

SEA SCALLOPS WITH CAPELLINI

Sea scallops are now available year-round, thanks to the grocer's freezer.
When they're tossed with ripe tomatoes and crisp bacon over angel hair pasta,
you have a feast for your eyes and your palate.

1/2 pound thick-sliced bacon, cut into 1/2-inch pieces
2 fresh garlic cloves, minced
1 pound sea scallops
3 cups heavy cream
2 tablespoons fresh thyme, stemmed
2 teaspoons paprika
1/2 teaspoon chili powder
1/2 teaspoon ground ginger
1/2 cup finely chopped peeled and seeded tomatoes
12 ounces capellini or angel hair pasta, cooked

Fry the bacon in a skillet over medium heat until crisp-cooked. Remove the bacon to a plate. Crumble the bacon. Drain the skillet, reserving 2 tablespoons of the drippings. Add the garlic to the reserved drippings and sauté for 1 minute or until softened. Add half the scallops and sear on both sides. Remove to a plate. Repeat the procedure with the remaining scallops. Pour the cream into the pan and cook over medium heat until reduced by 1/3, stirring frequently. Do not let the cream scorch. Stir in the thyme, paprika, chili powder and ginger. Add the tomatoes and scallops and cook until heated through. To serve, spoon the scallop sauce over the pasta. Sprinkle with the bacon.

Yield: 4 servings

GRILLED GROUPER WITH JALAPEÑO BUTTER

A native Florida fish and local favorite, grouper is a fast and flavorful solution to dinner. The Jalapeño Butter may be made ahead of time, wrapped tightly, and kept in the refrigerator for several days or frozen for up to one month. Wear rubber gloves when seeding and slicing the fresh jalapeño to avoid skin or eye irritation.

JALAPEÑO BUTTER
1 (3/4-inch) piece fresh gingerroot, peeled and cut into 1/4-inch slices
2 large fresh garlic cloves, cut into 1/4-inch slices
1 to 2 large fresh jalapeño chiles, seeded and sliced
1/4 cup coarsely chopped fresh cilantro
1/2 cup (1 stick) butter, softened

GROUPER
1 (11/2-pound, 1-inch thick) grouper fillet
Salt and pepper to taste
Lemon slices
Cilantro sprigs

For the butter, combine the gingerroot, garlic and jalapeño chiles in a food processor fitted with a steel blade and pulse until finely chopped. Add the cilantro and pulse to mix well. Combine with the butter in a small bowl and mix well. Wrap the mixture in plastic wrap or waxed paper and shape into a 6-inch log. Place in the refrigerator or freezer.

For the grouper, season the grouper with salt and pepper. Place on a greased grill rack or in a grill basket and grill over medium heat for 4 to 6 minutes for each 1/2-inch of thickness or until the fish flakes easily with a fork, turning once. You may broil the grouper 4 inches from the broiler for approximately the same amount of time if desired. Serve immediately with a slice of Jalapeño Butter and garnished with a slice of lemon and a sprig of cilantro.

Yield: 4 servings

PASTA PRIMAVERA WITH SMOKED SALMON

Prepare this dinner in one large stockpot. Serve it to your family in pasta bowls for a complete one-dish dinner. Smoked salmon and fresh vegetables make this a springtime treat!

1 pound asparagus, trimmed and cut into 1/2-inch pieces
8 ounces farfalle (bow tie pasta)
8 ounces (1 cup) sugar snap peas or snow peas
1/4 cup olive oil
3/4 cup grated Parmesan cheese
8 ounces smoked salmon, cut into thin strips
Salt and pepper to taste
Grated Parmesan cheese to taste

Cook the asparagus in boiling water to cover in a large stockpot for 3 to 5 minutes depending on the thickness of the stalks until tender-crisp. Remove the asparagus with a slotted spoon to a bowl filled with cold water. Let cool slightly; drain and set aside. Cook the pasta in the stockpot using the package directions, adding the sugar snap peas during the last 2 minutes of cooking time. The peas should be tender-crisp. Drain the peas and pasta and discard the water. Return the peas, pasta and asparagus to the stockpot and toss with olive oil to coat. Add 3/4 cup Parmesan cheese and the salmon and mix well. Season with salt and pepper and sprinkle with additional Parmesan cheese. Serve immediately.

Yield: 4 servings

Food and wine can both be accentuated when you consider matching flavors. Think of it the same way you might consider what side dish to serve with an entrée. Wine has subtle flavors like fruit, pepper, smoke, and herbs. Choose a wine that has a complementary effect, such as a toasty-oak chardonnay served with Pasta Primavera with Smoked Salmon.

SALMON WITH BROWN SUGAR AND MUSTARD GLAZE

A sweet and savory glaze makes this grilled salmon perfect for an afternoon cookout.

BROWN SUGAR AND MUSTARD GLAZE
1 tablespoon brown sugar
1 teaspoon honey
2 teaspoons unsalted butter
2 tablespoons Dijon mustard
1 tablespoon soy sauce
1 tablespoon olive oil
2 teaspoons peeled and grated fresh gingerroot

SALMON
1 (2 1/2-pound, 3/4- to 1-inch thick) whole salmon fillet

For the glaze, combine the brown sugar, honey and butter in a small sauté pan over medium heat and cook until melted, stirring frequently. Remove from the heat and whisk in the mustard, soy sauce, olive oil and gingerroot. Let stand until cool.

For the salmon, place the salmon skin side down on a large piece of foil. Trim the foil, leaving a 1/4- to 1/2-inch border. Coat the meat of the salmon with the glaze. Grill over medium heat until the edges begin to brown and the interior is opaque. Remove the salmon to a cutting board and cut crosswise into 6 to 8 pieces. Do not cut through the skin. Lift the meat from the skin using a spatula and arrange on a serving platter or individual plates. Serve immediately.

Yield: 6 to 8 servings

ROASTED SALMON WITH TOMATO CREAM SAUCE

Now that salmon fillets are so inexpensive, this is a dish perfect for the whole family or a last-minute gathering of friends. Serve this to the adults as the recipe directs and to children without the sauce if they prefer.

TOMATO CREAM SAUCE
1 tablespoon olive oil
2 shallots, minced
4 tomatoes, cored, seeded and chopped
1/2 cup heavy cream
1/2 cup thinly sliced fresh basil leaves

SALMON
1 tablespoon olive oil
4 (4-ounce) salmon fillets with skin
Kosher salt to taste

For the sauce, heat the olive oil in a 10-inch skillet over medium-high heat. Add the shallots and sauté until soft but not brown. Add the tomatoes and cook for 10 minutes or until most of the liquid is evaporated, stirring occasionally. Reduce the heat to low. Add the cream and cook just until heated through, stirring frequently. Remove from the heat.

For the salmon, preheat the oven to 325 degrees. Preheat a nonstick skillet over medium-high heat. Brush the olive oil over both sides of the salmon fillets. Place the salmon skin side down in the skillet and sear for 2 minutes on each side. Season with kosher salt. Place in a roasting pan or baking sheet with sides. Bake for 5 minutes or until the tip of a knife inserted in the center shows resistance.

To serve, warm the sauce. Stir the basil into the sauce. Spoon the sauce onto individual plates and top with the salmon.

Yield: 4 servings

BEEF TENDERLOIN WITH BLUE CHEESE AND PORT CARAMELIZED ONIONS

It is much more than a steak dinner when you add an elegant topping of blue cheese
and caramelized onions. This is an ideal dish for a small dinner party or any special occasion.

2 tablespoons unsalted butter
2 tablespoons vegetable oil
1 teaspoon brown sugar
1/4 teaspoon salt
3 sweet onions, cut into
    1/4-inch slices

1/3 cup port wine
4 (6- to 8-ounce) beef tenderloin steaks
Salt and pepper to taste
Worcestershire sauce to taste
4 ounces good quality blue cheese,
    crumbled

Heat the butter and oil in a large nonstick skillet over medium-high heat. Add the sugar, 1/4 teaspoon salt and onions and cook for 5 minutes or until the onion is soft, stirring occasionally. Reduce the heat to medium and cook for 35 minutes or until the onions are dark brown and sticky, stirring frequently. Stir in the port and cook for 5 minutes or until the onions are glazed. Reduce the heat to low.

Season the steaks with salt, pepper and Worcestershire sauce. Let stand at room temperature for 30 minutes. Grill over medium to medium-high heat to the desired degree of doneness, turning once. Remove from the grill and let stand for 5 to 10 minutes. Place the steaks on dinner plates and top with a generous amount of onions and crumbled blue cheese.

Yield: 4 servings

When looking for a wine to complement your food, try to match
weights. A light dish is best suited to a light wine—for example,
try Grilled Grouper with Jalapeño Butter (page 78) with a crisp
sauvignon blanc or riesling. Whereas a heavier, meaty dish like Beef
Tenderloin with Blue Cheese and Port Caramelized Onions would
pair well with a deep-flavored and balanced zinfandel.

GRILLED FLANK STEAK WRAPS

This flavorful wrap is a modern take on the roast beef sandwich with fabulous results.

1/4 cup soy sauce
2 tablespoons lemon juice
1 tablespoon Worcestershire
  sauce
2 fresh garlic cloves, crushed
1 tablespoon brown sugar
1/2 teaspoon ground ginger
1/4 cup vegetable oil
1 1/2 pounds flank steak
2 tablespoons olive oil

1 large onion, halved and sliced
1/4 teaspoon salt
1/2 cup boursin cheese, softened
1/4 cup mayonnaise
6 to 8 wraps or large flour
  tortillas
6 to 8 romaine lettuce leaves
8 ounces (2 cups) shredded
  Swiss cheese

Whisk together the soy sauce, lemon juice, Worcestershire sauce, garlic, brown sugar and ginger in a small bowl. Add the vegetable oil gradually, whisking until blended. Combine with the steak in a large resealable plastic bag. Marinate in the refrigerator for 2 to 12 hours.

Heat the olive oil in a large nonstick pan over medium heat. Add the onion and cook for 20 to 30 minutes or until golden brown, stirring frequently. Sprinkle with the salt.

Remove the steak from the marinade and discard the marinade. Grill over medium-high heat for 6 to 8 minutes on each side for medium rare. Remove from the heat and let cool. Cut into thin slices at a 45-degree angle across the grain.

Combine the boursin cheese and mayonnaise in a bowl and mix well. Spread 1 tablespoon of the mixture on each of the wraps, leaving a 1-inch border. Place a lettuce leaf on the lower 1/3 of each wrap. Top with the Swiss cheese and onions. Top each with 2 to 3 slices of the steak. Fold in the sides of the wrap and roll tightly to enclose the filling. May be chilled, wrapped in parchment paper or plastic wrap, for several hours before serving.

Yield: 4 to 6 servings

SAVORY BEEF SHORT RIBS OVER PAPPARDELLE

This dish will ward off any chills on a cool night. Pappardelle is a wide, flat noodle that may be purchased at specialty stores. If you cannot locate it in your area, you may substitute wide egg noodles.

4 pounds bone-in beef short ribs	1 cup beef stock
Salt and pepper to taste	1 cup red wine
2 tablespoons olive oil	1 (28-ounce) can tomatoes
1/2 cup chopped onion	2 sprigs fresh thyme, or
1/2 cup chopped celery	1 teaspoon dried thyme
1/2 cup chopped carrot	8 ounces pappardelle, cooked
2 fresh garlic cloves, minced	and drained
2 bay leaves	

Season the ribs with salt and pepper. Heat the olive oil in a wide, heavy ovenproof saucepan or Dutch oven over medium to medium-high heat. Add the ribs in batches and sear on both sides. Drain and discard all but 2 tablespoons of the drippings. Add the onion, celery and carrot to the drippings and sauté for 10 minutes or until the vegetables are soft. Add the garlic and sauté for 1 minute. Add the bay leaves, beef stock, wine, undrained tomatoes and thyme and mix well. Season with salt and pepper. Preheat the oven to 350 degrees.

Submerge the ribs in the liquid in a single layer in the bottom of the saucepan. Bake, covered, for 2 to 2 1/2 hours or until the meat is tender but not falling off the bone. Remove the ribs to a large platter and let stand, tented with foil. Strain the cooking liquid into a large bowl, pressing the solids to extract the liquid; discard the solids. Skim the fat from the surface of the liquid using a large spoon. Pour the liquid into a large saucepan and bring to a slow boil. Cook for 10 to 15 minutes or until thickened, stirring frequently. Pour over the ribs. Serve the ribs over the pasta.

You may prepare the ribs and sauce in advance and warm in the oven before serving. You may substitute Creamy Polenta (page 54) for the pasta if desired.

Yield: 4 to 6 servings

MOROCCAN MEATBALLS

We are always looking for a great recipe for this all-ages favorite! The herbs and spices make these meatballs extraordinary. Serve over rice or pasta for a complete meal.

1 pound ground beef
2 fresh garlic cloves, minced
1/4 cup stemmed and chopped
   fresh parsley
1/2 teaspoon cumin
1/2 teaspoon paprika
1/2 teaspoon ginger
1/4 teaspoon red pepper, or
   to taste

Salt and pepper to taste
2 tablespoons olive oil
4 large tomatoes, coarsely
   chopped
1 onion, chopped
1 (6-ounce) can tomato paste
3/4 cup warm water

Combine the ground beef, garlic, parsley, cumin, paprika, ginger, red pepper and salt and pepper in a large bowl and mix well. Shape into 1-inch balls. Heat the olive oil in a large skillet or saucepan over medium heat. Add the tomatoes and onion and sauté until the onion is tender. Combine the tomato paste and water in a small bowl and mix well. Stir into the tomato and onion mixture. Add the meatballs and simmer over medium to medium-low heat for 15 to 20 minutes or until cooked through. You may substitute a mixture of 1/2 pound ground beef and 1/2 pound ground lamb for the ground beef if desired.

Yield: 6 servings

"Cooking is like love. It should be entered into with abandon or not at all."

—Harriet Van Horne

BRAISED LAMB SHANKS

This savory ragout is wonderful for cool fall nights. It is best served over creamy polenta or grits. Once you have assembled the ingredients, it really cooks by itself. It may also be easily adapted to a slow cooker.

6 (3/4-pound) lamb shanks or
veal shanks
Salt and pepper to taste
3 tablespoons olive oil
1 large onion, diced
6 fresh garlic cloves,
finely chopped
3 carrots, diced
4 ribs celery, diced

1 (28-ounce) can diced tomatoes
in juice
2 1/4 cups chicken broth
3 sprigs fresh rosemary
3 sprigs fresh thyme
1 tablespoon freshly ground
pepper
Parmesan cheese

Season the lamb with salt and pepper. Heat 2 tablespoons olive oil in a large ovenproof saucepan over high heat. Add the lamb in batches and brown on all sides. Remove to a platter. Preheat the oven to 350 degrees. Heat the remaining 1 tablespoon olive oil in the saucepan. Add the onion, garlic, carrots and celery and sauté for 10 minutes or until the vegetables begin to brown and are softened. Add the lamb, undrained tomatoes, chicken broth, rosemary, thyme and 1 tablespoon pepper and bring to a boil.

Cover the pan and place in the oven. Roast for 2 hours or until the meat is tender and pulls easily from the bone. Remove the sprigs of rosemary and thyme and discard. Remove the lamb with a slotted spoon to a platter and let stand until cool to the touch. Remove the meat from the bones and coarsely chop. Bring the vegetable mixture to a boil and boil for 5 to 10 minutes or until the sauce is thickened, stirring frequently. Add the lamb and mix well. Serve over polenta or grits and sprinkle with Parmesan cheese.

To prepare in a slow cooker, brown the lamb and vegetables as directed above. Reduce the amount of chicken broth to 1 cup and combine all the ingredients in a slow cooker. Cook on High for 6 to 8 hours or until the lamb is tender. Remove the lamb and chop as directed above.

Yield: 4 to 6 servings

GRILLED HONEY-BOURBON PORK TENDERLOIN

Pork tenderloins are accented by the unusual pairing of bourbon, soy sauce, and ginger.
The marinade can be prepared the night before for a quick grilled meal.

1/2 cup chopped onion	1 tablespoon minced fresh gingerroot
1/2 cup lemon juice	4 to 5 fresh garlic cloves, minced
1/2 cup bourbon	2 tablespoons olive oil
1/4 cup honey	3 (12-ounce) pork tenderloins, trimmed
1/4 cup soy sauce	1/2 teaspoon each salt and pepper

Combine the onion, lemon juice, bourbon, honey, soy sauce, gingerroot, garlic and olive oil in a bowl and mix well. Place the pork in a large resealable plastic bag. Add the marinade and marinate in the refrigerator for 1 to 12 hours. The longer the pork marinates, the more flavorful. Remove the pork, reserving the marinade. Sprinkle the pork with the salt and pepper. Grill over high heat until a meat thermometer inserted in the middle of the pork registers 150 degrees, turning once and basting occasionally with the reserved marinade.

Yield: 8 to 10 servings

SAVORY SAUCE FOR GRILLED MEATS, POULTRY OR SEAFOOD

Combine 2 tablespoons sesame oil, 6 tablespoons dry white wine,

6 tablespoons soy sauce and 1/4 cup packed dark brown sugar

in a bowl and mix well. Combine with your choice of meat, poultry

or seafood in a large resealable plastic bag and marinate

in the refrigerator for 30 minutes or longer. Remove the meat and

discard the marinade. Yield: 1 1/8 cups, or enough to marinate

1 1/2 pounds meat, poultry or seafood.

CUBAN WRAPS

A traditional south Florida sandwich (much like a hero) wrapped up in a soft flour tortilla.

10 cloves roasted garlic
(page 49)
1/3 cup mayonnaise
1/3 cup mustard
4 (6- to 7-inch) flour tortillas
or wraps
4 large romaine lettuce leaves

4 ounces deli ham, thinly sliced
4 ounces roasted pork,
thinly sliced
4 ounces (1 cup) shredded
Swiss cheese
Sandwich-style sliced sour
pickles

Mash the garlic in a small bowl. Add the mayonnaise and mustard and mix well. Spread the mixture on the tortillas, leaving a 1/2-inch border. Place a lettuce leaf on the lower 1/3 of each tortilla. Top each with 1 ounce ham, 1 ounce pork, 2 tablespoons cheese and a pickle slice. Fold in the sides of the tortilla and roll tightly to enclose the filling. May be prepared several hours in advance and chilled, wrapped in parchment paper or plastic wrap, until ready to serve.

Yield: 4 wraps

For a personalized centerpiece at a family celebration, create a visual memory book by lining the center of the table with framed photos of the birthday boy or girl, or from the event if you're celebrating a role in a play or a big presentation. For a family reunion, find old photos of family members, enlarge them, and have everyone guess who is who. Decorate the table with items that reflect the passions and interests of those you are honoring, such as fishing lures for the avid fisherman, playbills for the Broadway fan, or cooking utensils or cookbooks for the food aficionado.

BREAKFAST BURRITO TO GO

1 slice bacon
1 egg
1 tablespoon water
1/2 tablespoon butter
1/4 teaspoon salt, or to taste

1 flour tortilla
2 tablespoons shredded Cheddar
cheese, Swiss cheese or
Monterey Jack cheese

Place the bacon between paper towels. Microwave on High for 1 to 2 minutes or until crisp. Combine the egg and water in a small bowl and mix well. Melt the butter in a small sauté pan over medium-high heat. Add the egg mixture and cook until firm. Sprinkle with the salt. Microwave the tortilla on High for 10 seconds. Sprinkle the cheese on the tortilla. Top with the egg and bacon and roll to enclose the filling.

Yield: 1 serving

TUSCAN FRITTATA

A frittata doubles as breakfast or a quick dinner. It is also an excellent way to use any leftover vegetables or meat that you have in your refrigerator.

8 to 10 eggs
1 teaspoon salt
Pepper to taste
3 tablespoons butter
1 onion, finely chopped
1/2 cup chopped sun-dried
tomatoes

1 cup (4 ounces) cubed smoked
mozzarella cheese or smoked
Gouda cheese
1 cup crumbled cooked Italian
sausage, drained
2 tablespoons fresh basil leaves,
thinly sliced

Preheat the oven to 400 degrees. Whisk together the eggs, salt and pepper in a large bowl. Heat the butter in a large nonstick ovenproof sauté pan over medium-high heat. Add the onions and cook until the onions are soft, stirring occasionally. Reduce the heat to medium. Combine the tomatoes, cheese and sausage with the eggs and mix well. Pour into the pan with the onions. Cook until the outside edge is set. Do not stir. Place the pan in the oven and bake for 15 to 20 minutes or until the top is slightly puffed and golden brown. Garnish with the basil and serve immediately.

Yield: 6 to 8 servings

SALTIMBOCCA

Chicken is topped with savory prosciutto, fresh sage, and fontina cheese for a quick but elegant main dish. This recipe will fool your friends into thinking you've been to cooking school!

4 boneless chicken breast cutlets
Salt and pepper to taste
4 (1-ounce) slices fontina cheese (optional)
8 fresh sage leaves
4 thin slices prosciutto
2 tablespoons flour
2 tablespoons olive oil
2 tablespoons butter
1/4 cup white wine
1 tablespoon butter

Place the chicken between 2 pieces of plastic wrap and flatten to 1/8-inch thick with a mallet. Season with salt and pepper. Place a slice of cheese on each cutlet. Top each with 2 sage leaves and 1 slice of prosciutto. Thread a wooden pick through the layers to secure. Sprinkle both sides lightly with the flour.

Heat the olive oil and 2 tablespoons butter in a large skillet over medium-high heat. Add the prepared chicken, prosciutto side down, and cook until golden brown, turning once. Remove the chicken to a platter and remove the wooden picks. Add the wine to the skillet and deglaze, scraping up the browned bits from the bottom of the skillet. Add 1 tablespoon butter and cook until blended. Pour the wine sauce over the chicken and serve immediately.

Yield: 4 servings

Classic Coq Au Vin

*This is a great dish to make on a Sunday afternoon, or make it early in the day and
cook it while you are at sports practice. It freezes well and is even better the next day.
This can easily be doubled for larger families or crowds.*

5 slices lean bacon, cut into
1/2-inch pieces
1 (31/2- to 4-pound) chicken,
skinned and quartered
1/2 teaspoon salt
1/4 teaspoon pepper
Flour
1 onion, finely chopped
10 pearl onions, peeled
2 large shallots, peeled and minced
1 head fresh garlic, cloves
separated and peeled

1/2 pound small mushrooms, sliced
2 tablespoons flour
1 teaspoon tomato paste
11/2 cups dry red wine such as pinot
noir
3/4 cup chicken stock or broth
6 sprigs fresh thyme
2 bay leaves
Salt and pepper to taste

Sauté the bacon in a large heavy Dutch oven over medium heat until crisp and brown. Remove the bacon with a slotted spoon to a plate. Season the chicken with 1/2 teaspoon salt and 1/4 teaspoon pepper. Coat lightly with flour, shaking off the excess. Brown in the bacon drippings over medium heat, working in batches so the chicken is not crowded in the pan. Remove to a platter. Preheat the oven to 350 degrees.

Add the onion, pearl onions, shallots and garlic to the pan and cook over medium heat for 5 to 10 minutes or until the onions are soft, stirring frequently. Add the mushrooms and cook until the mushrooms release their juices, stirring constantly. Add 2 tablespoons flour and the tomato paste and cook for 1 minute or until thickened, stirring constantly. Stir in the wine and chicken stock. Add the bacon, chicken, thyme and bay leaves. Season with salt and pepper. Bring to a boil and cover. Place in the oven and bake for 1 to 11/2 hours or until the chicken is tender and beginning to fall off the bone. Remove the thyme sprigs and bay leaves and serve with buttered noodles, rice or mashed potatoes.

Yield: 4 to 6 servings

WEEKNIGHT CHICKEN ENCHILADAS

This Tex-Mex favorite can be prepared ahead and served to a crowd. You'll find it perfect for post-practice, post-meeting weeknights, or a Saturday get-together with friends.

2 tablespoons vegetable oil
1 cup chopped onion
2 cups chopped peeled tomatoes
1/2 cup canned chopped green chiles
1 teaspoon ground cumin
1/2 teaspoon ground coriander
1 to 11/2 pounds boneless
skinless chicken breasts, cubed
3 tablespoons butter
1/2 cup chopped onion
2 to 3 fresh garlic cloves, minced
1/4 cup flour
1 cup chicken broth

11/2 cups milk
1/4 cup canned chopped green chiles
1 cup sour cream
1/2 cup (2 ounces) shredded
    Monterey Jack cheese
12 (6-inch) corn or flour tortillas
4 cups (16 ounces) shredded
    Monterey Jack cheese
2 cups (8 ounces) shredded sharp
    Cheddar cheese
Sour cream, chopped avocado,
    chopped fresh tomato

Heat the oil in a large skillet over medium heat. Add 1 cup onion and sauté until soft. Add the tomatoes, 1/2 cup green chiles, cumin and coriander and cook for 10 minutes, stirring occasionally. Add the chicken and simmer for 20 minutes or until the chicken is tender.

Melt the butter in a large sauté pan over medium heat. Add 1/2 cup onion and cook for 5 to 10 minutes or until the onion is translucent, stirring frequently. Add the garlic and cook for 1 minute. Add the flour and cook for 1 to 2 minutes, stirring constantly. Add the chicken broth and milk and cook for 5 minutes or until thick, stirring constantly. Add 1/4 cup green chiles, sour cream and 1/2 cup Monterey Jack cheese and mix well. Reduce the heat to low and simmer, covered, until ready for assembly.

To assemble and bake, preheat the oven to 350 degrees. Spoon several tablespoons of the chicken mixture on a tortilla. Top with 1 tablespoon each Monterey Jack cheese and Cheddar cheese. Roll to enclose the filling and place seam side down in a 9×13-inch baking pan sprayed with nonstick cooking spray. Repeat the procedure with the remaining tortillas, chicken mixture and cheese. Pour the sour cream sauce over the enchiladas. Sprinkle with 1 cup Monterey Jack cheese. Bake for 20 to 30 minutes or until heated through and bubbly. Serve with sour cream, avocado and chopped tomato. You may prepare the dish several hours in advance and keep chilled, covered, until ready to bake.

To prepare as a layered dish, cut the tortillas into fourths. Layer the tortillas, chicken mixture, sauce and cheese 1/2 at a time in a 9×13-inch baking dish sprayed with nonstick cooking spray. Bake as directed above.

Yield: 6 servings

GRILLED CHICKEN BROCHETTES

*A great chicken dish for the whole family. It assembles and cooks
quickly for a fuss-free weeknight dinner.*

1/2 cup olive oil
1/2 teaspoon ground cumin
1/2 teaspoon turmeric
Pinch of salt
1 pound boneless skinless chicken breasts, cut into 2-inch cubes

Combine the olive oil, cumin, turmeric and salt in a shallow dish and mix well. Add the chicken and turn to coat. Marinate in the refrigerator for 30 minutes. Soak wooden skewers in water for 30 minutes. Thread the chicken onto the skewers and discard the marinade. Grill over medium-high heat for 10 minutes or until cooked through, turning once.

Yield: 6 to 8 servings

SPICE RUB FOR MEAT, POULTRY AND FISH

For a quick and delicious way to enhance the flavors

of meat, poultry or seafood, combine 1 tablespoon brown sugar,

1 teaspoon sugar, 1 1/2 teaspoons cumin and 1 tablespoon each chili

powder, ground coriander and kosher salt in a small bowl and mix

well. Sprinkle over your choice of meat, poultry or fish and rub into

the surface. Roast in the oven or grill. The rub will keep stored in a

small jar or a resealable plastic bag. Double the recipe and save

the remainder for a last-minute meal solution.

CHICKEN STOCK

1 large roasting chicken
2 large onions, quartered
3 carrots, thickly sliced
3 ribs celery, thickly sliced

1 bunch fresh parsley
1 tablespoon kosher salt
2 teaspoons whole black
  peppercorns

Combine the chicken, onions, carrots, celery, parsley, kosher salt and peppercorns with water to cover by 3 to 4 inches in a large stockpot. Bring to a boil. Reduce the heat and simmer for 45 to 60 minutes or until the chicken is tender. Remove from the heat. Remove the chicken with 2 large slotted spoons to a dish to cool. Reserve the chicken for another use.

Strain the liquid through a fine mesh strainer and discard the solids. Use the stock immediately or let cool completely before storing. Chill for up to 3 days in the refrigerator or freeze for up to 2 months.

Yield: about 1 quart

MEDITERRANEAN TURKEY WRAPS

*Wraps are such an easy and convenient way to make a meal. These turkey wraps
are great for lunches, parties, and picnics.*

1/4 cup mayonnaise
4 (12-inch) wraps or tortillas
4 large romaine lettuce leaves
8 ounces turkey, thinly sliced
20 kalamata olives, pitted
  and chopped

6 tablespoons pine nuts, toasted
1/4 cup finely chopped roasted
  red peppers
1/4 cup stemmed and chopped
  fresh basil
4 ounces feta cheese, crumbled

Spread the mayonnaise over 1 side of each wrap. Place a lettuce leaf on the lower 1/3 of each prepared wrap. Layer the turkey, olives, pine nuts, red peppers, basil and feta cheese over the lettuce. Fold in the sides of the wrap and roll tightly to enclose the filling. Cut on the diagonal to serve. May be prepared several hours in advance. Wrap in parchment paper or plastic wrap and store in the refrigerator until ready to serve.

Yield: 4 servings

CRISPY DUCK BREASTS

Duck can be easy to prepare and an elegant alternative to chicken. Duck breasts may be found in the freezer section of most grocery stores. If you are short on time, you may make this dish without the chutney, and it will still be wonderful.

DUCK

4 boneless skin-on duck breast
halves, trimmed
1/2 teaspoon ground coriander

1/2 teaspoon salt
1/2 teaspoon pepper

PORT WINE SAUCE

1/3 cup tawny port wine
1/3 cup chicken broth
or water

1/2 teaspoon arrowroot
or cornstarch
1 tablespoon water

For the duck, pierce the skin of each duck breast several times using the tip of a knife. Season with the coriander, salt and pepper. Heat a large nonstick skillet over medium-high heat until hot. Place the duck skin side down in the skillet. Cook for 5 minutes; drain. Reduce the heat to medium and cook for 20 minutes or until the skin is crisp and golden, draining twice. Turn the duck over and cook for 5 to 7 minutes or until tender. Remove to a cutting board and let stand, tented with foil to keep warm. Drain the fat from the skillet.

For the sauce, heat the skillet over medium-high heat. Add the wine and bring to a boil, stirring with a wooden spoon to deglaze the skillet. Add the chicken broth and boil until reduced to about 1/3 cup. Combine the arrowroot and water in a small bowl and stir until the arrowroot is dissolved. Add to the wine mixture. Bring to a boil, stirring constantly. Remove from the heat.

To serve, cut each duck breast crosswise on the diagonal into slices. Arrange on 4 serving plates into a fan shape. Spoon the sauce over the top and serve with Fresh Mango Carrot Chutney (on page 54).

Yield: 4 servings

SWEET ENDINGS

BANANA DIPPERS

*A fun hands-on activity for the kids. Use this great idea for a
birthday party or a rainy day.*

8 ounces chocolate chips
4 bananas, cut into halves
1/2 cup colored sugar
1/2 cup chopped nuts
1/2 cup toasted coconut
1/2 cup ice cream sprinkles
1/2 cup crushed cookies
1/2 cup miniature "M&M's" chocolate candies

Place the chocolate chips in a microwave-safe bowl and microwave on High for 1 minute or until melted and smooth, stirring every 30 seconds. Skewer each banana half with a wooden popsicle stick. Dip the bananas in the chocolate. Roll in your choice of colored sugar, nuts, coconut, ice cream sprinkles, crushed cookies or chocolate candies. You may cut the bananas into smaller pieces and use wooden picks instead of popsicle sticks if desired.

Yield: 4 servings

"Food is our common ground, a universal experience."
—James Beard

BREAD PUDDING WITH VANILLA SAUCE

*This delicious comfort food is easy to make. The leftovers make an
indulgent breakfast or mid-morning snack.*

PUDDING

1 loaf stale French bread	3 eggs
4 cups milk	1^1/2 cups sugar
1 tablespoon unsalted butter, softened	2 tablespoons vanilla extract
	1 cup raisins or dried cherries

VANILLA SAUCE

^{1}/2 cup (1 stick) unsalted butter, softened
1 cup confectioners' sugar
1 egg, beaten
3 tablespoons vanilla extract or bourbon (or to taste)

For the pudding, cut the bread into cubes and place in a large bowl. Pour the milk over the bread and let stand for 1 hour. Preheat the oven to 325 degrees. Grease a 9×13-inch baking dish with the butter. Combine the eggs, sugar and vanilla in a mixing bowl and beat until blended. Pour over the bread mixture and mix well. Add the raisins and stir gently to combine. Spoon into the prepared baking dish. Bake on the middle rack of the oven for 60 to 70 minutes or until brown and set. Let stand until cool.

For the sauce, combine the butter and confectioners' sugar in a small saucepan over low heat. Cook until the confectioners' sugar is dissolved and the mixture is very hot, stirring frequently. Remove from the heat. Add the egg and whisk until the mixture has cooled to room temperature. Stir in the vanilla.

To serve, cut the pudding into squares and serve topped with the sauce. You may place the sauce-topped pudding under the broiler and broil until bubbling. Serve immediately.

Yield: 12 servings

APPLE CLAFOUTI

A clafouti is a warm fruit dessert made by topping a layer of fresh fruit with batter.

4 large apples, peeled, cored and
cut into 1/16-inch slices
1/2 cup sugar
1 teaspoon cinnamon
1/2 cup (1 stick) butter, melted

1 cup flour
1 teaspoon sugar
1/2 cup packed brown sugar
1/2 cup chopped pecans
(optional)

Preheat the oven to 350 degrees. Place the apples in an 8×8-inch baking pan sprayed with nonstick cooking spray. Combine 1/2 cup sugar and the cinnamon in a small bowl and mix well. Pour over the apples. Combine the butter, flour, 1 teaspoon sugar, brown sugar and pecans in a bowl and mix well. Spread evenly over the apples. Bake for 45 minutes. Serve warm or at room temperature with ice cream or whipped cream. For a more crisp-like dessert, cut cold butter into the dry ingredients with your fingertips, two knives or a food processor. Sprinkle over the apples and bake as directed.

Yield: 6 to 8 servings

MAPLE MOUSSE

Using a high-quality syrup will give you the best results with just a hint of maple flavoring.

4 egg yolks
11/4 cups high-quality grade-A
maple syrup

1 pint whipping cream
4 egg whites

Beat the egg yolks in a small bowl. Combine with the maple syrup in the top of a double boiler and mix well. Cook over boiling water for 15 to 20 minutes or until the mixture is thick and silky and coats the back of a spoon, whisking constantly. Remove from the heat and let stand until cool. Whip the cream in a mixing bowl. Beat the egg whites until stiff peaks form in a small bowl. Fold into the whipped cream. Fold in the cooled maple syrup mixture. Pour into a serving dish or individual parfait glasses. Chill for several hours before serving. You may freeze in individual cups before serving.

Note: This recipe contains raw egg whites. To avoid raw eggs that may carry salmonella, you may use an equivalent amount of pasteurized egg substitute.

Yield: 12 servings

MASCARPONE FRUIT TART

This tart is quick to make! Your friends will be fooled into thinking you're a pastry chef.

1 (1-crust) pie pastry, or 1 baked Pâte Brisée (below)
8 ounces mascarpone cheese
2 tablespoons confectioners' sugar
2 tablespoons rum
Sliced fresh fruit

Fit the pie pastry in a tart pan and bake using the package directions. Remove from the oven and let stand until cool. Combine the mascarpone, confectioners' sugar and rum in a bowl and beat until smooth. Spread over the cooled tart crust. Top with your favorite sliced fruit. Slice and serve.

Yield: 6 servings

PÂTÉ BRISÉE

Not your ordinary pie pastry!

1¹/2 cups sifted unbleached flour
¹/2 teaspoon salt
¹/2 cup (1 stick) unsalted butter, cubed
¹/4 cup ice water

Combine the flour and salt in a bowl. Cut in the butter with a pastry blender until the mixture resembles coarse crumbs. Add the ice water 1 tablespoon at a time and mix just until the dough holds together. Turn the dough out onto a lightly floured surface and knead with the heel of your hand. Shape the dough into a ball and knead several times. Shape into a disk and chill, wrapped in plastic wrap, for 30 minutes. Place on a lightly floured surface and roll out into a 12-inch circle. Fit into a tart pan and bake at 375 degrees for 10 to 15 minutes or until light golden brown.

Yield: 1 pâté brisée

CHOCOLATE TORTE

*This torte is an elegant, make-ahead dessert. Top with fresh raspberries and
whipped cream or place in a pool of Quick Raspberry Sauce (page 105).*

4 eggs
1 tablespoon sugar
1¹/2 cups (3 sticks) unsalted butter
1 pound semisweet or sweet chocolate
1 tablespoon flour

Preheat the oven to 325 degrees. Spray an 8-inch springform pan with nonstick cooking spray
and line the bottom with parchment paper. Press foil tightly over the outside bottom and side of
the pan to prevent leaks.

Combine the eggs and sugar in a mixing bowl and beat on high for 5 minutes or until light yellow
and fluffy. Combine the butter and chocolate in a large heatproof bowl. Set the bowl over simmering
water and heat until blended, stirring frequently. Remove the bowl from the heat and fold in the egg
mixture gently, 1/3 at a time. Sprinkle with the flour and fold in gently. Be careful not to deflate the
batter. Pour into the prepared springform pan and set the pan in a 9×13-inch baking pan. Add boiling
water to reach halfway up the side of the springform pan. Bake for 25 minutes or until the edge is puffed
but the center still jiggles. Remove to a wire rack to cool. Remove the side from the pan and chill,
covered, for 8 hours before serving.

Yield: 12 servings

If you want to enjoy a special wine with dessert, make

sure to choose one that is sweeter than the dessert, or the wine will

taste bitter. Try a sparkling wine or champagne, a sweet

Muscat or tawny port, with our Chocolate Torte for a

wonderful ending to a memorable meal.

GINGERBREAD CAKE WITH FRESH ORANGE GLAZE

Your home will smell like fall! Kids will love this cake served as a dessert or snack.

CAKE

2 tablespoons butter, softened
2 tablespoons sugar
2 1/2 cups flour
2 teaspoons baking powder
1/2 teaspoon salt
1/4 teaspoon baking soda
1 teaspoon cinnamon
1/4 teaspoon nutmeg
1/4 teaspoon ground cloves

1/2 cup dark molasses
1/2 cup milk
1 1/4 cups (2 1/2 sticks) unsalted butter, softened
1 1/4 cups packed brown sugar
3 tablespoons chopped crystallized ginger
4 eggs, at room temperature

FRESH ORANGE GLAZE

1 tablespoon unsalted butter, melted
2 tablespoons milk
1/4 teaspoon vanilla extract

Juice of 1/2 orange (about 2 to 3 tablespoons)
1 teaspoon grated orange zest
1 cup confectioners' sugar

For the cake, preheat the oven to 350 degrees. Grease the bottom and side of a 10- to 12-cup bundt pan with 2 tablespoons butter. Sprinkle with the sugar. Combine the flour, baking powder, salt, baking soda, cinnamon, nutmeg and cloves in a bowl. Combine the molasses and milk in a small bowl and mix well. Cream 1 1/4 cups butter and the brown sugar in a mixing bowl until light and fluffy. Add the ginger and mix well. Add the eggs 1 at a time, beating well after each addition. Add the mixture of dry ingredients alternately with the molasses mixture, beginning and ending with the dry ingredients and beating at low speed after each addition until smooth. Pour into the prepared pan. Bake for 50 minutes or until the side pulls away from the pan and a wooden pick inserted near the center comes out clean. Cool on a wire rack for 10 minutes. Invert onto a serving plate to cool completely.

For the glaze, combine the butter, milk, vanilla, orange juice and orange zest in a medium bowl and whisk until blended. Whisk in the confectioners' sugar, adding additional confectioners' sugar if desired for a thicker consistency. Pour over the cooled cake.

Yield: 16 servings

VANILLA LAYER CAKE WITH BUTTERCREAM ICING

Our large and impressive layer cake is great for a birthday party or special gathering.

CAKE

1 cup (2 sticks) unsalted butter, softened	1^1/$_2$ cups self-rising flour
	1^1/$_4$ cups all-purpose flour
2 cups sugar	1 cup milk
4 eggs, at room temperature	2 teaspoons vanilla extract

BUTTERCREAM ICING

1 cup (2 sticks) unsalted butter, softened	1/4 teaspoon salt
	3 tablespoons milk
3 cups confectioners' sugar	1^1/$_2$ tablespoons vanilla extract

For the cake, preheat the oven to 350 degrees. Spray two 9-inch cake pans with nonstick cooking spray and line the bottom of each pan with parchment paper. Cream the butter in a mixing bowl. Add the sugar and beat at medium speed for 2 to 3 minutes or until light and fluffy. Add the eggs 1 at a time, beating well after each addition. Combine the self-rising flour and the all-purpose flour in a bowl. Add to the creamed mixture alternately with the milk and vanilla, beginning and ending with the flour mixture and beating well after each addition. Pour into the prepared pans. Bake for 25 to 30 minutes or until golden brown, the sides are pulling away from the pans and a wooden pick inserted near the center comes out clean. Remove to a wire rack for 10 minutes. Invert the cakes onto the wire rack to cool completely.

For the icing, cream the butter in a mixing bowl. Add the confectioners' sugar, salt, milk and vanilla and beat at medium speed for 2 to 3 minutes or until smooth. Spread the icing between the layers and over the top and side of the cooled cake. You may add 1 tablespoon grated orange or lemon zest to the icing for a citrus-flavored icing if desired.

To make cupcakes, spoon the batter into 24 paper-lined muffin cups, filling them 3/4 full. Bake at 350 degrees for 20 minutes or until a wooden pick inserted near the center comes out clean.

Yield: 12 cake servings or 24 cupcakes

ONE BOWL POUND CAKE

This moist pound cake is prepared in only one bowl. Another
plus is that it keeps for several days.

2¹/2 cups flour
2 cups sugar
¹/2 teaspoon baking soda
¹/4 teaspoon salt
1 cup (2 sticks) butter, softened
1 (8-ounce) container lemon or vanilla yogurt
1 teaspoon vanilla extract
4 eggs

Preheat the oven to 350 degrees. Grease and flour a 10-inch bundt pan. Combine the flour, sugar, baking soda, salt, butter, yogurt, vanilla and eggs in a large mixing bowl and beat at low speed until blended. Beat at medium speed for 3 minutes. Pour into the prepared pan. Bake for 60 to 70 minutes or until golden brown and a wooden pick inserted near the center comes out clean. Serve with Quick Raspberry Sauce (below).

Yield: 8 servings

QUICK RASPBERRY SAUCE

Purée 1 (12-ounce) bag of defrosted frozen raspberries

in a blender. Pour through a strainer into a bowl, pressing on the

solids with the back of a spoon to extract all of the juice. Stir in 4 to

5 tablespoons confectioners' sugar and mix well. Chill, covered,

until ready to serve. Yield: 1¹/3 cups.

PEACH POUND CAKE

A refreshing fruit-filled twist on a classic recipe.

3 cups flour
1 teaspoon baking powder
1/2 teaspoon salt
1 cup (2 sticks) butter, softened
2 cups sugar
4 eggs
1 teaspoon vanilla extract
2 cups chopped peaches

Preheat the oven to 325 degrees. Grease a 10-inch bundt pan generously with butter and sprinkle with sugar, shaking out the excess. Combine the flour, baking powder and salt in a bowl. Cream the butter and sugar in a mixing bowl until light and fluffy. Add the eggs 1 at a time, beating well after each addition. Add the vanilla and beat well.

Add the flour mixture gradually, beating constantly until blended. Fold the peaches into the batter. Spoon into the prepared bundt pan. Bake for 60 to 70 minutes or until golden brown and a wooden pick inserted near the center comes out clean. Cool in the pan for 10 minutes. Invert onto a wire rack to cool completely.

Yield: 8 to 10 servings

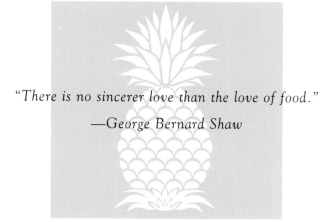

"There is no sincerer love than the love of food."
—George Bernard Shaw

CHOCOLATE CHEESECAKE

Our tasters loved this sweet, chocolaty alternative to the traditional cheesecake.

CHOCOLATE CRUST
15 chocolate sandwich cookies
1/2 cup chopped pecans
3 tablespoons unsalted butter, melted

FILLING

24 ounces cream cheese, softened	5 ounces semisweet chocolate, melted
1¹/2 cups sugar	1 teaspoon vanilla extract
2 tablespoons flour	1/4 cup milk
3 eggs	Whipped cream

For the crust, preheat the oven to 325 degrees. Line the bottom of a 9-inch springform pan with waxed paper. Combine the cookies and pecans in a food processor fitted with a steel blade and pulse until the consistency of fine crumbs. Combine with the butter in a small bowl and mix well. Press over the bottom and slightly up the side of the prepared pan. Bake for 6 minutes. Remove from the oven and let stand until cool.

For the filling, combine the cream cheese, sugar and flour in a food processor fitted with a steel blade and process until blended. Add the eggs 1 at a time, pulsing after each addition. Add the chocolate, vanilla and milk and pulse until blended. Pour into the baked crust. Place the pan on a large baking sheet with sides. Bake for 60 minutes or until the center is set. Cool on a wire rack for 45 minutes. Remove the side of the pan and chill, covered, for 5 to 8 hours. Serve with whipped cream. You may freeze the cheesecake, wrapped tightly in plastic wrap, for up to 1 month.

Yield: 12 to 14 servings

BLUEBERRY PIE

Summer berries never had it so good!

4 cups (2 pints) fresh blueberries
1 cup sugar
3 tablespoons flour
1/2 teaspoon grated lemon zest
Dash of salt
1 (2-crust) pie pastry, or 1 recipe
Pâte Brisée (page 101)

1 cup crushed butter cookies
1 to 2 teaspoons lemon juice
1 tablespoon butter
3 tablespoons milk
2 tablespoons sugar

Preheat the oven to 400 degrees. Combine the blueberries, 1 cup sugar, flour, lemon zest and salt in a bowl and gently toss to mix. Unfold 1 pie pastry into a pie plate. Fit into the plate and trim the edge. Sprinkle the cookie crumbs over the pastry. Pour the blueberry mixture over the cookie crumbs. Drizzle with the lemon juice and dot with the butter. Top with the remaining pastry, sealing the edge and cutting vents. Brush the top with the milk and sprinkle with 2 tablespoons sugar. Bake for 35 to 40 minutes or until golden brown. To prevent the edge from browning too quickly, you may cover with foil. Serve with vanilla ice cream.

Yield: 8 servings

TROPICAL PECAN PIE

A sweet treat that has the taste of the islands.

2 eggs
1/2 cup (1 stick) butter,
  melted
1 cup sugar
1/2 cup shredded coconut
1/2 cup chopped pecans

1/2 cup golden raisins
1 teaspoon vanilla extract
1/4 teaspoon white vinegar
1 unbaked (9-inch) pie shell, or
  1 recipe Pâte Brisée
  (page 101)

Preheat the oven to 300 degrees. Beat the eggs slightly in a bowl. Add the butter, sugar, coconut, pecans, raisins, vanilla and vinegar and mix well with a spoon. Pour into the pie shell. Bake for 50 to 55 minutes or until the filling is set.

Yield: 8 servings

OLD-FASHIONED VANILLA ICE CREAM

This recipe comes from the kitchen of a League Member who is a culinary professional. We were thrilled she would share it with us!

3 cups half-and-half	3/4 cup sugar
6 egg yolks	2 teaspoons vanilla extract

Bring the half-and-half to a low simmer in a heavy saucepan over medium heat, stirring occasionally. Do not let it boil over. Combine the egg yolks and sugar in a metal mixing bowl and whisk until blended. Pour 1 cup of the half-and-half into the egg mixture gradually, whisking constantly. Pour the egg mixture into the remaining half-and-half. Cook over medium-low heat for 3 to 7 minutes or until slightly thickened and a finger drawn across the back of the spoon leaves a path, stirring constantly with a wooden spoon to ensure that lumps do not form. Do not boil. Remove from the heat and pour into a bowl. Chill, covered, in the refrigerator for 1 hour up to 3 days. Stir in the vanilla. Pour into an ice cream freezer container and freeze using the manufacturer's directions. Spoon into a storage container and freeze until firm. Serve with Chocolate Fudge Sauce (below).

Yield: 1 quart

CHOCOLATE FUDGE SAUCE

This versatile sauce may be served over ice cream and brownies, used as a chocolate fondue base with cubed pound cake and fresh fruit, or eaten right out of the pan when no one is looking!

1 cup semisweet chocolate chips	1 (12-ounce) can evaporated
1/2 cup (1 stick) unsalted butter	milk
2 cups confectioners' sugar	1 teaspoon vanilla extract

Combine the chocolate chips and butter in the top of a double boiler and heat until blended, stirring frequently. Pour the mixture into a medium saucepan. Stir in the sugar and evaporated milk. Bring to a low boil over medium heat and boil for 8 minutes or until the sauce has thickened, stirring frequently. Remove from the heat and stir in the vanilla extract.

Yield: about 4 cups

FLORIDA ORANGE COOKIES

Inspired by an old Florida recipe, this is a rich, buttery, cake-like cookie.

COOKIES

1 cup (2 sticks) butter	2 eggs
2 cups sugar	5 cups flour
4 ounces freshly squeezed orange	2 teaspoons baking powder
juice (from 1 1/2 oranges)	1 teaspoon baking soda
2 tablespoons grated orange zest	1 cup buttermilk

ORANGE ICING

2 cups confectioners' sugar	3 tablespoons freshly squeezed
1/4 cup (1/2 stick) butter,	orange juice
softened	1 teaspoon grated orange zest

For the cookies, preheat the oven to 350 degrees. Cream the butter and sugar in a large bowl until light and fluffy. Add the orange juice and orange zest and mix well. Add the eggs and beat until blended. Combine the flour, baking powder and baking soda in a bowl. Add to the creamed mixture alternately with the buttermilk, mixing well after each addition. Drop the dough by 1/4 cups 1 inch apart onto a greased or parchment paper-lined cookie sheet. Bake for 14 minutes or until golden brown. Remove to a wire rack to cool completely. For smaller cookies, drop by teaspoonfuls and bake for 11 to 12 minutes.

For the icing, combine the confectioners' sugar, butter, orange juice and orange zest in a bowl and mix well, adding additional orange juice to reach the desired consistency. Spread over the cooled cookies.

Yield: 3 dozen cookies

LACE COOKIES WITH CHOCOLATE FILLING

*These thin, crisp, and delicate cookies are easy to assemble and
were popular with young testers.*

3/4 cup (1 1/2 sticks) butter, melted	1/2 teaspoon vanilla extract
1 1/2 cups packed brown sugar	1 1/2 cups rolled oats
1 egg, beaten	1 cup semisweet chocolate pieces, melted

Preheat the oven to 350 degrees. Cream the butter and brown sugar in a bowl until light and fluffy. Add the egg and vanilla and mix well. Fold in the oats. Drop by teaspoonfuls 2 inches apart onto a parchment paper-lined or foil-lined cookie sheet. Bake for 8 to 10 minutes or until golden brown. Cool slightly on the cookie sheet. Remove carefully to a wire rack to cool completely. The cookies will be very fragile. Spread a small amount of chocolate over the flat side of half the cooled cookies. Top with the remaining cookies, flat side down, to form a sandwich.

Yield: 2 dozen cookies

MONSTER COOKIES

3/4 cup (1 1/2 sticks) butter, softened, or shortening	1 tablespoon vanilla extract
1 1/4 cups packed dark brown sugar	2 teaspoons baking soda
1 cup sugar	4 1/2 cups quick-cooking oats
3 eggs	1/2 cup chocolate chips
12 ounces (1 1/2 cups) peanut butter	1/2 cup chopped walnuts or pecans
	1/2 cup raisins

Preheat the oven to 350 degrees. Cream the butter, brown sugar and sugar in a bowl until light and fluffy. Add the eggs 1 at a time, beating well after each addition. Add the peanut butter, vanilla, baking soda and oats and mix well. Stir in the chocolate chips, walnuts and raisins. Drop by large spoonfuls onto a nonstick cookie sheet. Bake for 12 to 15 minutes or until golden brown. Remove to a wire rack to cool.

Yield: about 5 dozen cookies

MILK CHOCOLATE MACADAMIA NUT COOKIES

Milk chocolate chunks and toasty macadamia nuts are the highlight
of these big and chewy cookies.

1 cup (2 sticks) unsalted butter, softened
1 cup packed brown sugar
1 cup sugar
2 eggs
2 teaspoons vanilla extract
2$1/2$ cups flour
1 teaspoon baking soda
1 teaspoon salt
8 ounces milk chocolate, coarsely chopped
1 cup coarsely chopped macadamia nuts

Preheat the oven to 325 degrees. Cream the butter, brown sugar and sugar in a large bowl until light and fluffy. Add the eggs and vanilla and mix well. Combine the flour, baking soda and salt in a bowl. Add to the creamed mixture and mix well. Stir in the chocolate and macadamia nuts. Drop by 1/4 cups 2 inches apart onto a parchment paper-lined cookie sheet. Bake for 17 to 18 minutes or until light brown and set in the center. Remove to a wire rack to cool completely.

You may prepare the cookie dough in advance and refrigerate for several hours. Spoon 1/4 cups of the dough in single layers into resealable freezer bags and freeze until ready to bake. To bake, increase the baking time by 2 to 3 minutes.

For a chocolate and white chocolate chunk version, add 3 ounces melted semisweet chocolate to the creamed mixture and 1/4 cup cocoa to the dry ingredients and substitute 8 ounces semisweet chocolate chunks for the milk chocolate and 8 ounces chopped white chocolate for the macadamia nuts.

Yield: 3 to 5 dozen cookies

SUGAR COOKIES

Testers voted this cookie dough the easiest to work with, producing delicious cookies in fun shapes.

COOKIES

1 cup (2 sticks) unsalted butter, softened	1 teaspoon vanilla extract
	1/2 teaspoon almond extract
1 cup sugar	3 3/4 cups flour, sifted
2 eggs	3 teaspoons baking powder
1 tablespoon milk	1/4 teaspoon salt

VANILLA ICING

1/2 cup water	5 cups confectioners' sugar, sifted
1/4 cup light corn syrup	1 teaspoon vanilla extract

For the cookies, cream the butter and sugar in a bowl until light and fluffy. Add the eggs, milk, vanilla extract and almond extract and mix well. Sift the flour, baking powder and salt into a bowl. Add to the creamed mixture and mix well. Divide the dough into halves. Shape each half into a disk and chill, wrapped in plastic wrap, for several hours or until firm.

Preheat the oven to 375 degrees. Roll 1 dough disk 1/8 inch thick on a lightly floured surface, sprinkling the dough and rolling pin with additional flour as needed. Cut with a cookie cutter dipped in flour and arrange 1 inch apart on an ungreased cookie sheet. Bake for 8 to 10 minutes or until light brown. Remove to a wire rack to cool. Repeat the procedure with the remaining dough.

For the icing, combine the water and corn syrup in a medium saucepan over medium-high heat and bring just to a boil. Remove from the heat and stir in the confectioners' sugar and vanilla until smooth. Pour into a medium bowl. Dip the top side of the cookies into the icing, allowing the excess to drip off. Invert onto a wire rack. You may add your choice of food coloring and citrus zest to change the color and flavor of the icing.

Yield: 4 dozen cookies

PEANUT BUTTER BARS

A kid-friendly snack that may be eaten right out of the refrigerator
accompanied by a cold glass of milk.

BARS
1 cup (2 sticks) butter, softened
1 cup packed brown sugar
1 cup sugar
2 eggs
2 teaspoons vanilla extract
2 cups flour
1 cup rolled oats
1 1/2 cups creamy peanut butter

CHOCOLATE ICING
1/4 cup (1/2 stick) butter
6 tablespoons cocoa powder
1/2 cup milk
1 pound confectioners' sugar

For the bars, preheat the oven to 325 degrees. Cream the butter, brown sugar and sugar in a mixing bowl until light and fluffy. Add the eggs and vanilla and beat until blended. Add the flour and oats and mix well. Spread evenly in a 10×15-inch buttered baking pan. Bake for 25 minutes or until light brown and set in the center. Spread the peanut butter over the warm crust. Let stand until cool.

For the icing, melt the butter in a saucepan over medium heat. Add the cocoa and milk and mix well. Add the confectioners' sugar and whisk until smooth. Spread over the cooled peanut butter layer. Chill, covered, for several hours before serving. Store in the refrigerator.

Yield: 60 bars

EASY CHOCOLATE TRUFFLES

An elegant, sweet treat at the end of a meal or the perfect gift. Kids can make their own version by rolling the truffles in colored sprinkles!

8 ounces semisweet chocolate, chopped
4 ounces cream cheese, softened
2 1/4 cups confectioners' sugar, sifted
1 teaspoon vanilla extract
1/4 cup sifted cocoa powder, chocolate sprinkles or finely chopped hazelnuts

Place the chocolate in a non-reactive bowl. Microwave on High just until melted, stirring every 30 seconds. Combine the cream cheese and confectioners' sugar in a bowl and mix well. Add the chocolate and vanilla and mix well. Shape into small balls. Roll in the cocoa powder, chocolate sprinkles or hazelnuts. Place on a waxed paper-lined tray and chill for 2 hours or longer.

Yield: about 1 dozen

QUICK KEY LIME CURD

For a quick and easy dessert, this can be poured over fruit, into a pie shell, or spread between cake layers. When folded into whipped cream, it makes a fluffy citrus mousse.

1/2 cup (1 stick) butter
1/2 cup sugar
1/4 cup fresh lime juice or key lime juice
Grated zest of 1 lime
3 eggs

Combine the butter, sugar, lime juice and lime zest in a glass bowl. Microwave, covered tightly with plastic wrap, on High for 4 minutes. Stir until blended. Beat the eggs in a bowl. Whisk 1/4 cup of the lime mixture into the eggs. Add the egg mixture to the lime mixture gradually, whisking constantly. Microwave, uncovered, on High for 4 minutes, whisking well after 2 minutes. Pour into a blender or food processor and process for 30 seconds or until smooth. Let stand until cool.

Yield: 4 to 6 servings

Menus

Last-Minute Dinner for Drop-In Friends

Garlic Cheese Spread *with crackers*

Roasted Salmon
with Tomato Cream Sauce

Garlic Green Beans

Quick Key Lime Curd *with
shortbread cookies and raspberry garnish*

Weekend Dinner for Two or a Group

Braised Lamb Shanks

Creamy Polenta

Mixed greens with dressing and
Croutons

Old-Fashioned Vanilla Ice Cream with
Chocolate Fudge Sauce

Weekend Lunch for a Crowd

Tomato Soup

Pita Triangles *or* Popovers

Really Good Chicken Salad *over
field greens*

Blueberry Pie

Slow Cook Winter Supper

Field greens with
Lemon Dijon Vinaigrette

Classic Coq au Vin

Bread Pudding with Vanilla Sauce

Items in italics are suggestions. Use your favorite recipe or store brand.

Menus

Quick Dinner for a Weeknight

Saltimbocca

Broccoli with Goat Cheese

Buttered noodles

One-Bowl Pound Cake

Portable Dinner for a Friend

Fresh Carrot Salad

Grilled Honey Bourbon Pork Tenderloin

Lemon Rice

Florida Orange Cookies

Friday Afternoon Drinks with Family and Friends

Red Rockets

Lemonade

Roasted Bar Nuts

Brie with Herbs in a Baguette

Green Olive Tapenade *with crackers*

Assorted vegetables and ranch dressing

MEASUREMENT EQUIVALENTS

1 tablespoon = 3 teaspoons
2 tablespoons = 1 ounce
4 tablespoons = 1/4 cup
51/3 tablespoons = 1/3 cup
8 tablespoons = 1/2 cup
12 tablespoons = 3/4 cup
16 tablespoons = 1 cup
1 cup = 8 ounces or 1/2 pint
4 cups = 1 quart
4 quarts = 1 gallon
1 (61/2- to 8-ounce) can = 1 cup
1 (101/2- to 12-ounce) can = 11/4 cups
1 (14- to 16-ounce) can = 13/4 cups
1 (16- to 17-ounce) can = 2 cups
1 (18- to 20-ounce) can = 21/2 cups
1 (29-ounce) can = 31/2 cups
1 (46- to 51-ounce) can = 53/4 cups
1 (61/2- to 7-pound) can = 12 to 13 cups

FREEZING TIPS

- List the date on all items before placing them in the freezer.
- Freezing canned hams or processed meats is not recommended. Frozen canned hams become watery and soft when thawed. Processed meats have a high salt content, which causes them to become rancid at a quicker rate during the thawing process.
- Do not freeze stuffed chickens or turkeys. The stuffing may become contaminated with bacteria during the lengthy thawing process.
- Partially thawed food that still has ice crystals in the package can be safely refrozen. A safer test is to determine if the surface temperature is 40 degrees Fahrenheit or lower.

SPECIAL THANKS

A cookbook is a collaboration of many people. To all those listed, we thank you sincerely for your part in this endeavor. We have made every effort to express gratitude to everyone who has touched this project. If we have inadvertently left your name out, please accept our sincerest apologies.

To those families who so graciously gave us access to their beautiful homes for the photos in this cookbook:

Thilo and Betsy Best and Family
Saade and Gail Chibani
Frank and Paula Perry
Alton and Mary Esther Parker
The neighbors of South Willow Avenue in
Historic Hyde Park

To the businesses that allowed us access to props and settings for the photographs in this cookbook:

Alvin Magnon Jewelers
Magnolia Furnishings, Gifts and Objects of Charm
The Arrangement Florist
The Garden Party
Villa Rosa Distinctive Linens and Bath Shop

RECIPE CONTRIBUTORS

A special thank you to our many recipe contributors, who submitted their treasured recipes and favorite foods. Although we could not use them all, each was unique and wonderful . . .

Laura Allegri	Patti Cowart	Rebecca Jo Garbrick
Carole Anderson	Monica Culpepper	Joyce Gerwe
Anne Arthur	Colleen Crosby	Laura Lee Glass
Christy Atlas	Laurie Doerr Daigle	Amy Goldsmith
Gabrielle Ayala	Carrie DaRe	Betsy Graham
Joanne Moore Baldy	Kristen Karig Day	Beverly Bacon Gray
Kristen Barrett	Leigh Ann Dempsey	Donna Hall
Paige Barry	Connie Detrick	Kim Harcrow
Jennifer Bommarito	Terrie Dodson	Beth Harris
Jacque Bordonali	Tweed Cline Eckhard	Elizabeth Harris
Alexis Borucke	Alysia Ekizian	Joy Harty
Greta Brooks	Jeni Eldridge	Janell Harvey
Chris Holt Brown	Helen D. Erb	Susan Hawkins
Helen Thompson Brown	Laura Estes	Vicki Hayes
Jill Buhler	Mary E. Estes	Cyrilla Helm
Claire Burgess	Gina Fair	Melissa Henry
Caroline Burt	Laura Farrior	Megan Hernandez
Julie Byrd	Laurin Farrior	Lynne Hildreth
Liz Agan Caiello	Robyn Fedorovich	Michelle Hogan
Jen Carlstedt	Bruce Flatten	Penny Hulbert
Ginger Caruso	Gail Frank	Joelle Hunter
Maia Chrisman	Brittain Fraser	Maria Fe Inga
Lelia Clewis	Cheryl B. Fraser	Lynn Isaak
Gina Colley	Laura Darrow Frost	Susan Isbell
Ansley Cowart	Lisa Gabler	Cynthia Janko

Nina Jennings
Jennifer Jesski
Leigh Kaney
Lynn Kelyman
Meagan Kempton
Anne Mullen Kutchmire
Deanna Laird
Elizabeth Lambert
Dara Leslie
Winifer MacKinnon
Jennifer McQueen
Lisa McRae
Connie Meadows
Nancy Mellon
Michelle Miller
Peggy Miller
Jennifer Mitchell
Phyllis Mitchell
Melissa Moran
Julie Muroff
Mindy Murphy
Nancy H. Mynard
Sallie Nardone
Catherine Pacifici
Paula Perry
Chris Phillips

Vanessa Fava Pivec
Corey Poe
Kathleen Purdy
Jane Ramos
Beth Ransom
Theo Renaud
Tara Richardson
Lindsey Robbins
Cheryl Rodriguez
Dianne Rossi
Eleanor Rossi
Franci Rudolph
Carla Rudy
Brittany Rustman
Kristie Salzer
Cynthia Sanders
Lauren Satterwhite
Karyn Sbar
Michelle Schofner
Gretchen Sebring
Meeghan Seoane
Stephanie Shaw
Sarah Spicola
Jodi Spitz
Lynn Stanford
Sarah Stichter

Janice Straske
Elayne Suber
Elaine Sweeney
Jennifer Tanck
Julie Tate
Susan Taulbee
Kathleen Thaxton
Holly Thomas
Sarah Trice
Jen Tsarrett
Leanne Voiland
Cherie Ward
Teresa Weachter
Angela Weck
Lisa Robinson Weiss
Lisa Williams
Theresa Wresh
Lou Yates
Laura York

RECIPE TESTERS

With appreciation to our faithful testers, who opened their kitchens and gave us invaluable feedback . . .

Ekecia Allen	Gina Colley	Sally Hardee
Charlee Alvarez	Lauren Cooper	Beth Harris
Gwen Anderson	Abby Cronin	Elizabeth Harris
Lisa Andrews	Laurie Cuva	Susan Hawkins
Nicole Andriso	Laurie Doerr Daigle	Heather Hays
Christy Atlas	Carrie DaRe	Cyrilla Helm
Lee Ellen Banks	Kim Daxon	Lynne Hildreth
Danelle Barksdale	Pam Divers	Sally Hill
Cheryl Benitez	Terrie Dodson	Lisa Hodgdon
CeCi Berman	Tweed Cline Eckhard	Michelle Hogan
Stacey Bessone	Karla Edwards	Joellyn Holt
Hedy Bever	Alysia Ekizian	Margaret Holzer
Jacque Bordonali	Jeni Eldridge	Tara Hoss
Alexis Borucke	Laura Estes	Maritza Iacono
CeCe Bowman	Gina Fair	Maria Fe Inga
Jennifer Brenner	Laura Farrior	Lynn Isaak
Wendy Brill	Cindi Feingold	Sue Isbell
Christine Brown	Amber France	Nina Jennings
Julie Brown	Jeanine Frederick	Peggy Jones
Christine Bruno	Vivienne Fu	Gina Jung
Allison Burden	Lisa Gabler	Leigh Kaney
Christina Burden	Suzanne Gabler	Michelle Kaney
Claire Burgess	Corinne Gaertner	Debbie Kavouklis
Laurie Ann Burton	Ashlie Gardner	Meagan Kempton
Julie Byrd	Susan Gear	Julie Kite-Powell
Liz Agan Caiello	Kathy Gibson	Lauri Kleman
Ashley Carl	Betsy Graham	Lynne Koeniger
Jen Carlstedt	Stacy Gramling	Deanna Laird
Ginny Charest	Donna Hall	Elizabeth Lambert
Britton Cisneros	Kim Harcrow	Suzanne Lehner

Dara Leslie
Brenda Little
Jen Brandt Little
Winifer MacKinnon
Jennifer Maekos
Peggy Maloney
Jennifer Markus
Beth Martinez
Stacey Matthews
MaryAnne McDonough
Jessica McIntyre
Joan McKay
Jennifer McQueen
Lisa McRae
Nancy Mellon
Nicole Melone
Kelli Mitchell
Yoon-Sook Moon
Melissa Moran
Mindy Murphy
Carol Nichols
Tina Nunn
Jennifer Patterson
Paula Perry
Catalina Pieper
Ann Pilecki
Carolyn Piper
Ashley Porcaro
Lori Pucci-Rey
Kathleen Purdy

Irene Quisenberry
Amie Ragano
Jane Ramos
Audrie Ranon
Beth Reid
Marnie Renda
Alison Reteneller
Janice Rickert
Mary Riding
Kristi Riggio
Christina Roberts
Kristen Rocha
Christine Romer
Lori Root
Dianne Rossi
Michelle Rowe
Carla Rudy
Kristie Salzer
Catherine Sanders
Michelle Schofner
Alicia Schumacher
Gretchen Sebring
Meeghan Seoane
Meghan Sheil
Angie Short
Paula Sincell
Angie Sparks
Katie Springman
Julie Stead
Kathy Stephens

Sarah Stichter
Janice Straske
Kathy Sulzer
Upik Suwarno
Jennifer Tanck
Courtney Tanis
Julie Tate
Susan Taulbee
Kathleen Thaxton
Anna Thayer
Susan Thompson
Marianne Touger
Sarah Travis
Taryn Tschetter
Lisl Unterholzner
G. G. Van Aelst
Shalle VanHorn
Beth Vickburg
Cherie Ward
Teresa Weachter
May Weber
Angela Weck
Danielle Welsh
Heather Werry
Lisa Williams
Stacy Williams
Laura Woodard

INDEX

EVERYDAY FEASTS

The Junior League of Tampa, Inc.
87 Columbia Drive • Tampa, Florida 33606
813-254-1734 extension 502
www.jltampa.org

YOUR ORDER	QUANTITY	TOTAL
EveryDay Feasts at $17.95 per book		$
The Life of the Party at $17.95 per book		$
JLT Culinary Collection at $31.95 (includes *The Life of the Party* and *EveryDay Feasts* cookbooks)		$
Shipping and handling at $4.95 for one book; $2.00 for each additional book		$
	Subtotal	$
Florida residents add 7% sales tax		$
	TOTAL	$

Name _____

Address _____

City _____ State _____ Zip _____

Telephone _____

Method of Payment: [ ] VISA   [ ] MasterCard
                   [ ] Check payable to The Junior League of Tampa

Account Number _____ Expiration Date _____

Signature _____

Photocopies will be accepted.